1994

The Glass-House Years

The Glass-House Years

Victorian Portrait Photography

1839-1870

ELIZABETH HEYERT

Allanheld & Schram / George Prior

MONTCLAIR AND LONDON

for M & D

Published in the United States of America in 1979
by ALLANHELD, OSMUN & CO.
19 Brunswick Road, Montclair, N.J. 07042
and by ABNER SCHRAM LTD.
36 Park Street, Montclair, N.J. 07042
Distribution: Abner Schram Ltd.

Published in the United Kingdom in 1979
by George Prior Associated Publishers Ltd.
37-41 Bedford Row
London WC1R 4JH

ISBN 0-86043-199-1

Library of Congress Cataloging in Publication Data

Heyert, Elizabeth
   The glass-house years.

Bibliography: p.
Includes index.
1.   Photography—Great Britain—History.   2. Photo
2.   Photography—Portraits.   I.   Title.
TR57.H49   779'.2'0941   77-25432
ISBN 0-8390-0214-7

Printed in the United States of America

Contents

Foreword and Acknowledgments

This is a book about the first thirty years of portrait photography in Great Britain, and its purpose is to put this aspect of photography into the context of history. It is a social history rather than a technical one, and the subjects of the book are the photographers, their sitters, and their critics.

That the first generation to experience photography would trust implicitly in its authenticity does not seem strange to us, because in the early days the public knew what the camera could do, but not what it could not do. Today we are aware how sadly the descriptive powers of the camera can disappoint us, how elegantly the camera can lie, and how pointedly it can reveal and distort. Yet, in viewing the portrait photographs of history, we seem to retain a naive trust in the objectivity and accuracy of the camera. We know the Victorians from their photographs and choose to think this is how they really were. In this book we shall explore some of the psychological burdens affecting the sitter and the social pressures facing the photographers in an effort to separate the fact and fiction concerning the portraits of history. In addition, the book attempts to formulate a method of criticism for historical photographs.

For permission to reproduce material I am indebted to the artists, collectors, and museums who have kindly allowed their work to be reproduced. I am grateful to the Royal Photographic Society, London, for permission to use their facilities, and I wish to thank their librarian Leo de Freites and Gail Buckland for their help. Thanks are due to Dr. John Hedgecoe, Head of Photography at the Royal College of Art, London, and Michael Langford, Senior Tutor in Photography, Royal College of Art, for their guidance. I extend special thanks to Aaron Scharf for his interest and encouragement, as well as for his valuable advice.

List of Illustrations

The Glass-House Years

1

The New Portraitists

On the 19th of August, 1839, an audience at the Institut de France listened in stunned silence to details about a miraculous new invention that would faithfully record what the eye could see. Addressing a joint meeting of the Academies of Science and Beaux Arts, Deputy François Arago made this claim on behalf of the inventor L. J. M. Daguerre:

> The daguerreotype does not demand a single manipulation which is not perfectly easy to every person, requires no knowledge of drawing, and does not depend on any manual dexterity. By observing a few simple directions, anyone may succeed with the same certainty and perform as well as the author of the invention. . . [1]

Within days, a special committee was established to investigate the value of the new invention, and were told by spokesman Gay-Lussac: ". . . the process is the origin of a new art in the midst of an old civilization, an art which will constitute an era and be preserved as a title of glory. . ."[2]

The dramatic announcement and thunderous publicity that resulted were orchestrated by Louis Jacques Mandé Daguerre, a theatrical designer and co-inventor of the Diorama. His process was to a great extent "borrowed" from heliography, invented by Nicéphore Niépce, who had produced the first fixed photographic image in 1826. Niépce became Daguerre's partner and communicated the details of his direct positive on metal process to him. After Niépce's death, Daguerre refined the original heliograph process by reducing exposure from eight hours to from five to twenty minutes and introduced daguerreotypy to the public as the first practical method of photography.[3]

1

With his patron Arago's aid, Daguerre was able to persuade the French government to purchase the rights to his invention, in order (he claimed) to insure the world free access to it. Daguerre received a large sum of money for the daguerreotype process, but soon after the public announcement, the French government realized they were victims of a clever confidence scheme. Five days before concluding the sale, Daguerre had taken a patent out for his invention in England under the pseudonym of Miles Berry of Chancery Lane—not only for the manufacture of the camera, but also for the manufacture and exhibition of all daguerreotype pictures.[4] "Miles Berry" was promptly taken to court, and the indignant editors of the London *Art-Union* told their readers: "M. Daguerre claims the exclusive right over his invention—M. Daguerre has got into the Court of Chancery."[5]

The court case against Daguerre proceeded with a deliberation worthy of *Jarndyce vs. Jarndyce* of Dickens's *Bleak House*,[6] and, meanwhile, aspiring English daguerreotypists were forced to seek Daguerre's permission to experiment with the new process, and to pay a stiff patentee fee.

The public quickly discovered that the original claims for the daguerreotype were exaggerated. While the process succeeded admirably with landscape and still life, human likeness still could not be reproduced. Light acted on the iodized plate so slowly that posing for a portrait was tortuously difficult, requiring the sitter to remain immobile for twenty to thirty minutes. If the subject moved during the exposure time, he was blurred and in some cases actually obliterated from the picture, and the long exposures that were required made movement inevitable.[7]

Chemists and opticians experimented with improvements stimulated both by the daguerreotype's potential for portraiture and by a desire to circumvent Daguerre's patent. Two Americans, Alexander Woolcott and John Johnson, succeeded in October 1839 in producing an image using a concave mirror rather than a lens.[8] Early in 1840, Johnson's father, William S. Johnson, introduced from America a mirror camera which produced pictures 2 x 2½ inches. Continuing to experiment in partnership with an Englishman named Richard Beard, they achieved a significant shortening of exposure time. The *Morning Chronicle* reported:

> All the difficulties which were in the way of the application of this principle to the taking of portraits have been overcome by a gentleman by the name of Woolcott, a native, we believe, of New York, who has substituted for the camera of Daguerre, a metallic speculum, and has also introduced the use of large reflecting mirrors for the purpose of illuminat-

ing the features in such a way as to give a proper degree of light and shade to the countenance. By this new process the time required for a person to sit for his portrait is reduced so under different circumstances of the light, likenesses may be taken in from one to four minutes.[9]

Woolcott's partner, Richard Beard, who was a coal merchant and part-time inventor, obtained patent rights from Daguerre for "Improvements in Apparatus for Taking Or Obtaining Likenesses and Representations of Nature and of Drawings and Other Objects" on June 13, 1840. In the patent he describes, in addition to Woolcott's improvements, a new method of varying the degree of light and shade in the portrait by the use of reflectors and semi-transparent screens.

Almost simultaneously, M. Antoine Claudet, a Frenchman working in London as a glassmaker, devised a method for accelerating the production of the original daguerreotype. Claudet discovered in 1841 that if the silver plate were sensitized by a combination of chlorine and iodine, rather than iodine alone, the sensitivity to light could be increased to such an amazing degree that Daguerre's lens became suitable for portraiture. Claudet and Beard soon became fierce competitors as daguerreotype portrait photographers. With Claudet's competition in mind, Beard advertised his own portraits as "inimitable"; Claudet characterized Beard as a "wideawake speculator."

Beard opened the first public photographic portrait studio in Europe in March, 1841, at the Royal Polytechnic Institution in London (Figure 1). He was shrewd enough to realize that the novelty of the new process would only sustain its commercial value if the public were given somewhat satisfactory results. The mirror camera that he used required exposure times from three seconds in summer to two minutes in winter, and the caricature of the tortured sitter, strapped to his chair with his neck in a vice, was receiving considerable publicity in *Punch* and other magazines. Alexander Woolcott had attempted to alleviate some of the sitter's discomfort by devising a system of liquid filters to protect the sitter's eyes from the glare, but found the arrangement impractical for a large public studio. Beard refined Woolcott's idea, designing a circular studio lighted from above by a flat roof of blue glass. This "glass-house," which allowed the photographer enough light for a reasonable exposure time but subdued the glare of the sun's rays so that sitters were not afflicted by watering eyes, was adopted by almost every portrait photographer in Europe. In June, 1841, Claudet set up a glass-house studio on the roof of the Royal Adelaide Gallery, a popular scientific center in competition with the Royal Polytechnic, and soon glass-houses were so prevalent that one London

Figure 1. Richard Beard's Trade Card. Richard Beard established the first daguerreotype photographic studio in England. (Science Museum, London)

"... It appears ... that M. Daguerre claims the exclusive right over his invention in England. ... Upon what ground he proceeds we are at a loss to guess; for the pension he received from the French government was expressly assigned to him because no such exclusive right could be maintained ..."

—*The Art-Union*, 1839

"DAGUERREOTYPE PORTRAITS taken daily at the Gallery of Practical Science, Adelaide Street ... by the improved process of Mr. A. Claudet, which requires but a few seconds to obtain a perfect Likeness. By this process also, pictures forming groups of three to six persons can be taken, either engaged at tea, cards, chess, or in conversation . . . Messrs. Claudet and Houghton, No. 89, High Holborn."

—*The Athenaeum*, July 17, 1841

Figure 2. A Lady. A very early daguerreotype, possibly taken by Richard Beard. (Science Museum, London)

5

"Amongst all the mechanical poison this terrible 19th century has poured on men, it has given us at any rate one antidote—the daguerreotype. Its a most blessed invention, that's what it is."

—John Ruskin

"Could we now see in Photogenic light and shade Demosthenes launching his thunders at Macedon, or Paul preaching in Athens, with what rapture should we gaze upon impersonations so exciting. The heroes and sages of ancient times would thus have been embalmed with more than Egyptian skill."

—*Edinburgh Review*

Figure 3. Early daguerreotype by Antoine Claudet. Portrait of the inventor Andrew Pritchard, July 18, 1843, one-ninth plate. (Victoria and Albert Museum, London)

street where a number of portrait studios were located became known as Glasshouse Street and remains so to this day.

Beard solved the problem of physical discomfort, but he and his associates still had to wrestle with the problem of psychological uneasiness. The glass-house roof cast an unearthly, almost ghostlike light on to the faces of visitors, which caused one visitor to Beard's studio to remark, "the livid paleness of complexion visible in the faces of the persons assembled caused a strange sensation."[10] Anxiety about the result of a sitting was intensified by the technically poor images which often resulted when an overcast sky made the light weak. In spite of Beard's improvements, the sitter was still forced to use a headrest, similar to ones used by Sir Thomas Lawrence and other portrait painters, and to remain motionless during the highly technical operation:

> The apparatus used was a rectangular box; at one end inside was fixed the concave mirror, the other being open to the sitter. . . . The operator having made all his arrangements, not forgetting the posing of the sitter, the sensitized plate was handed to him out of the darkroom, he tells the sitter what he is going to do, throws a dustcloth over the open end of the rectangular box, opens a small door in it opposite the pedestal, introduces his hand with the box and plate; he lifts the focussing glass out of the frame, puts the silver tablet in its place; withdraws his hand from the empty box, closes the door, withdraws the cloth from the front of the box and exposes. The exposure lasts from three to five minutes.[11]

Advertisements of the period for portraits by "the mirror of nature" added to the sitter's anxiety—the photographer, who was considered merely the operator of the machine, could not be blamed for an unflattering or comical portrait. Unlike the sitter for a commissioned painted portrait, who relied on the artist for an attractive picture, the first sitters at a photographic studio believed the camera produced an exact likeness, and many were horrified by the images of themselves that resulted. An anecdote captioned "A Fitting Error" in an early photographic magazine reflects the fear of some early sitters of appearing ridiculous:

> A gentleman felt very uncomfortable a week or so ago when, on going to sit for his photograph, he was asked by the artist, who was by no means happy in his pronunciation in some of his words, whether he wished to have his "fool-face" taken. . . .[12]

One of the most difficult problems seemed to be maintaining a relaxed expression, particularly during the long period necessary for exposure. The

INTERESTING GROUP POSED FOR A DAGUERREOTYPE

By a Friend of the Family.

INTERESTING AND VALUABLE RESULT.

From *Punch in Cameraland*, W. & J. Mackay & Co. Ltd, Chatham, 1948.
Courtesy *Punch Magazine*.

sitter was invited to "call up a look of pleasurable animation"—not an easy expression to maintain with any degree of naturalness for periods of one to five minutes. In the resulting portrait, which technical problems usually prevented from "mirroring nature," the intensity of the shadows often made the features look massive and exaggerated details of facial shape, so that the sitter looked even more uncomfortable than he actually was.

Early practitioners tried to alleviate the sitter's psychological discomforts by developing a kind of "bedside manner." Manuals for prospective portrait photographers advised the photographer to "cultivate an appearance that would inspire confidence, all elements of a gentleman (particularly courtesy), great patience and good temper, a refined and keen perception of mind in all its phases, and the ability to see at once to what type each form belonged (so as to give prominence to those physical attributes of the individual)"; and more, the photographer had to be "full of general information in order to converse with every person on his own favorite theme!"[13]

Although portrait photography flourished as a business, the public was slow to take it seriously. At the Royal Polytechnic Institute, Beard's photographic show took its place along side such "freak" inventions as "LONGBOTTOMS PHYSIOSCOPE which exhibits the human face with its varied expressions on a gigantic scale, curiously contrasted with the living man . . ."[14] Popular skepticism grew because the technical quality of many early attempts at portraiture was poor, and the results were often unpredictable. A reporter described several daguerreotypes that clients cancelled as unacceptable:

> They were persons who had very red faces, which looked black and heavy; from which we infer that the redness of the lips contributes to give the mouth that dark tint, that, added to the strong shadow between and below the lips makes this feature look larger and coarser than life . . .[15]

There were other problems. *The Art-Union* in 1842 complained of the "coldness of tone" of daguerreotype portraits. One reporter called daguerreotype portraits "unflattering to disagreeableness;" another wrote:

> . . the grave look and formal attitude commonly assumed by the sitters, being faithfully reflected in the miniature portrait, the somber effect of the strong shadows and colorless lights of the photograph is increased to an unpleasing degree of sternness, occasionally amounting to a repulsiveness, and, sometimes, even falsifying the likeness . . .[16]

Both Beard's method and Claudet's for taking daguerreotype portraits had drawbacks. Beard's process was the quicker of the two but the total time required to produce a portrait was about the same, because Claudet took two different views of the face at once in two cameras, while Beard took two in succession in the same camera. The daguerreotype produced a positive image that could not be reproduced, so that photographers had to repeat the entire procedure for each image. Beard's method had one obvious advantage over the process used by Claudet. Although the amount of distortion of the image in the refracting medium used by Claudet was less than that of the reflector used by Richard Beard, the image transmitted through Claudet's lens was reversed. The reversal of features had a far more damaging effect on the fidelity of the likeness than the distortion produced by Beard's reflector. Claudet did employ a parallel mirror with which he claimed he could take a portrait either way when he found faces not alike on both sides.[17]

Many daguerreotype photographers admitted the difficulty of achieving an accurate yet attractive delineation of the face. "An Amateur" in a letter appearing in the *Art-Journal* wrote:

Figure 4. Plans for Richard Beard's glass-house studio, 1840 (Patent office, London). Drawing after original plans by David Bentheim.

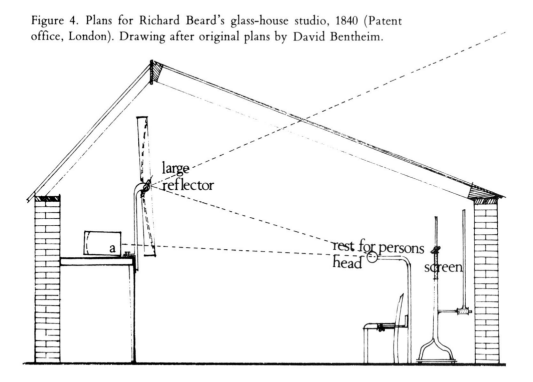

> I have tried to take likenesses, but I must acknowledge that the sun is no
> flatterer, and that the features which, under the pencil of Ross or Paris
> would be beautiful, are, to say the least, far from attractive . . . .[18]

Claudet, who was more successful, also stressed the difficulties involved to
enhance his own accomplishments—or perhaps to forestall criticism of the
inevitable failures. Thomas Sutton, editor of *Photographic Notes,* remembers
being harangued by Claudet in the latter's newly opened glass-house on the
roof of the Royal Adelaide Gallery:

> M. Claudet informed me, with the utmost gravity, that to achieve
> anything like success or eminence required the chemical knowledge of a
> Herschel, the artistic talent of a Reynolds or Rembrandt, the indomitable
> pluck and energy of a Hannibal, and under the circumstances he strongly
> advised against anyone taking it up as an amusement. I thought of the
> assistant who had really executed the practical part of taking my pic-
> ture. . . .[19]

In spite of results that were often unsatisfactory, the novelty of the idea
caught on quickly with a public intrigued by any new invention from mould
candles that "Burn Without Snuffing" to castor oil preparations for stimu-
lating the growth of hair. Photography immediately became a lucrative
business for its growing ranks of practitioners. As early as 1841, this new
species of portraiture could earn for the photographer, as was the case at
Beard's studio, an average of £150 per day—a sum that included income from
the sale of expensive cameras, frames, and nicknacks. The price was small for
the narcissistic pleasure of seeing one's own face immortalized in a lasting
record for posterity.

Daguerreotypes were made in standard sizes. Daguerre's favorite size
appears to have been 6½″ × 8½″, the largest size which could be taken with the
earliest cameras. This size was called the whole plate.[20] Other sizes were
fractions of this, i.e. half-plate (4½″ × 6½″), quarter-plate (3¼″ × 4¼″), one-
sixth plate (3¾″ × 3¼″), and one-ninth plate (2″ × 2½″).[21]

The public's avid desire for portraits was the major stimulus to improvements in the photographic process. During the early 1840s many inventions
related to portraiture were devised for producing lenses and cameras to enable
the photographer to meet the growing demand. In 1839 the most suitable lens
for photography was the single landscape lens, which could be used at
apertures up to about f/15. It covered a field of about fifty feet. The great
disadvantage to the single landscape lens was the long exposure time demanded

by the small aperture. In 1840 a Hungarian mathematician named Joseph Petzval produced a portrait lens which could be used at apertures as large as f/3.5—twenty times as fast as the single landscape lens.[22] The development of this lens marked a turning point for portrait photographers.

At the time Daguerre made his process public, Fox Talbot, a scientist, mathematician and linguist from Lacock, had already discovered a way to make paper sensitive to light. Talbot communicated his discovery to the Royal Society on January 31, 1839 and shortly afterwards, in the *London and Edinburgh Philosophical Magazine,* he described the process of preparing paper for making photogenic drawings, and for the calotype. The photogenic drawing process

Sitter. " OH, I THINK THIS POSITION WILL DO, IT'S NATURAL AND EASY."
Photographer. " AH, THAT MAY DO IN ORDINARY LIFE, MA'AM ; BUT IN PHOTOGRAPHY IT'S OUT OF THE QUESTION ENTIRELY ! "

From *Punch in Cameraland,* W. & J. Mackay & Co. Ltd, Chatham, 1948. Courtesy *Punch Magazine.*

"The most transitory of things, a shadow, the proverbial emblem of all that is fleeting and momentary, may be fettered by the spells of our 'natural magic' and may be fixed forever in the position which it seemed only destined for a single instant to occupy. . ."

—Fox Talbot, "On the Art of Fixing a Shadow"

Figure 5. Fox Talbot, daguerreotype by Antoine Claudet. At one time judged by Sothebys, London, to be the most valuable daguerreotype in existence, 2¾″ × 3¼″, (Royal Photographic Society, London)

Figure 6. Two calotypes showing W. H. F. Talbot's Printing Establishment at Reading. This photographic printing establishment was the first in the world, opened by Talbot in 1844. For three years, thousands of calotypes were produced there for book illustration and for sale in stationer's shops. The two calotypes, which combine to give panorama,

show some of the activities—copying engravings, taking portraits, printing positives from calotype negatives, and calotyping still life. The establishment closed in 1847. (Ref: Science Museum photography catalogue, 1969) (Science Museum, London) consisted of exposing sensitized paper in a tiny camera until an image appeared. The image was obtained after thirty to ninety minutes, and, unlike the daguerreotype, it was a negative image. In 1835 Talbot began to make positives by placing the negative in contact with a second sensitized piece of paper and exposing the new sheet to light transmitted by the negative. In his announcement concerning "the new art of photogenic drawing," Talbot made particular mention of its use for portraiture:

> Another purpose for which I think my method will be found very convenient is the making of outline portraits or silhouettes. These are now often traced by hand from shadows projected by a candle. But the hand is liable to err from the true outline, and a very small deviation causes notable diminution in the resemblance. I believe that this manual process cannot be compared with the truth and fidelity which the portrait is given by means of solar light.[23]

The main drawback of Talbot's photogenic drawing process was the long time necessitated to expose the image. Talbot suspected that a latent image might be drawn out by application of the proper chemical, and on September 23, 1840, he recorded the development of an image on paper apparently blank, with gallic acid:

> The . . . exciting liquid* was diluted with an equal bulk of water, and some very remarkable effects were obtained. Half a minute suffices for the camera. The paper when removed is blank but when kept in the dark the picture begins to appear *spontaneously,* and keeps improving for several minutes, after which it should be washed and fixed. . .[24]

The new process reduced exposure time from about one hour to one to two minutes, making portraiture practical. Talbot named his discovery the "Calotype" (from the Greek *kalos* meaning "beautiful") but his friends and even critics called the process the "Talbotype."

---

*A sheet of paper was sensitized with gallo-nitrate of silver (gallic acid, silver nitrate and acetic acid), then exposed to light in a camera for one to three minutes. The apparently blank sheet was developed by a further treatment of gallo-nitrate of silver.

Figure 7. Two calotypes. (Science Museum, London) *(top)* Calotype portrait of a lady. *(bottom)* Calotype portrait of Mary Russell Mitford, 3″ × 4″.

Thomas Moore, the Irish poet, writes in his memoirs:

"August 18, 1841 . . . started for Lacock Abbey this morning on my way to town. The day beautiful and I found grouped upon the grass before the house Kit Talbot, Lady E. Fielding, Lady Charlotte, and Mrs. Talbot for the purpose of being photogenized by Henry Talbot who was busily preparing his apparatus. Walked alone for a while about the gardens, and then rejoined the party to see the result of the operation. But the portraits had not turned out satisfactorily, nor oddly enough were they all like, whereas a dead likeness is, the sure though frightful result of Daguerre's process . . ." (Ref: D. B. Thomas, *The First Negatives*, London, 1964, p. 12.)

Figure 8. A calotype by Talbot showing a group at Lacock Abbey, c. 1844. (Science Museum, London)

Figure 9. Chess players, a calotype by Talbot, c. 1844. (Science Museum, London)

In *The Pencil of Nature,* a manual describing the uses of the calotype process, Talbot discusses its application to portraiture:

> . . . . when a group of persons has been artistically arranged, and trained by a little patience to maintain an absolute immobility for a few seconds of time, very delightful pictures are easily obtained. I have observed family groups are especial favourites: and the same five or six individuals may be combined in so many varying attitudes, as to give much interest and a great air of reality to a series of pictures. What would not be the value to our English Nobility of such a record of their ancestors who lived a century ago? On how small a portion of their family picture galleries can they rely with confidence![25]

Talbot's insight into the potential application of portrait photography was unusual for the period. The notion of photographic portraiture as a record for posterity was not seriously considered until Herbert Fry undertook to produce a "National Gallery of Photographic Portraits" fifteen years later, and Fry's attempts were considered radical even for his decade. Talbot's position as a landed gentleman, and his many intellectual accomplishments, placed him in a favorable position to influence public opinion about the serious practical and creative potential of the photography. He was a member of Parliament at the time he began to experiment with the camera obscura (1833-34), after attending Harrow and Trinity College, Cambridge, from which he was graduated with honors. Photography was only one of Talbot's numerous interests. In 1831 he was elected a Fellow of the Royal Society for his achievements in mathematics. He also made an exhaustive study of the origins of words and published a book entitled *English Etymologies,* and was one of the original translators of the Assyrian cuneiform inscriptions, with Sir Henry Rawlinson and others.[26] No matter how skeptical critics were about the possibility that photography might one day be regarded less as a gimmick than as a fine art, or at least a practical science, Talbot's invention was greeted with respectful interest.

By 1845 *The Art-Union* was reporting the perfection of Talbot's calotype process for portraiture:

> We have called attention more than once to the really wonderful results of Mr. Talbot's invention, now known by the above name [the Talbotype]. The invention is applied to portraiture by M. Claudet at the Royal

Adelaide Gallery, who has arrived at a high degree of perfection and certainty in producing portraits by this process . . .[27]

The calotype, although devoid of the delicacy and sharpness of the daguerreotype, had distinct advantages especially for portraits. Some photographers, for example the Scottish painter and photographer David Octavius Hill, exploited the sacrifice of realistic detail for creative purposes. He wrote of the calotype in 1848: "The rough surface and unequal texture throughout of the paper is the main cause of the calotype failing in details, before the process of the Daguerreotype—and this is the very life of it. They look like the imperfect work of a man—and not the much diminished work of God."[28]

The calotype seemed to answer the public demand for likenesses by reconciling accuracy and softness, providing portraits that were, like paintings, accurate up to a point. (Most daguerreotypists compensated for the unflattering realism of the daguerreotype image by employing a miniature painter to remove some of the truthfulness of the portrait, by removing blemishes, widening the eyes, and painting out flaws. The results had more the appearance of miniature paintings than photographs.) In addition to answering the critics' desire to see "artistic" likenesses, the calotype yielded a limitless number of identical prints.

The first professional calotype portraitist was Henry Collen, who remained Queen Victoria's favorite miniature painter for most of her life. Collen's calotypes were so heavily retouched that they resembled sketches—the images that remain today are actually pen drawings since the calotype image has faded entirely. The earliest surviving calotype portrait of Queen Victoria, taken by Collen around 1844 or 1845, shows her posed with the Prince of Wales. Collen, who abandoned calotypy in less than a year, made his most significant contribution to photography with his experiments in stereoscopic portrait photography. Stereoscopic photography, the impression of a third dimension obtained by simultaneously viewing two pictures taken from a slightly different viewpoint, was rarely attempted during the early stages of photography. Photographers found it nearly impossible to obtain two consecutive pictures without movement during the extended exposure time. Collen overcame this problem with a lens developed by Thomas Ross, fast enough to accomplish two exposures in a reasonably short time, but even Collen grew discouraged by numerous mistakes and failed to pursue stereoscopy for long. The process was to become a commercial success for future portrait photographers.

Figure 10. Dr. Boyd (specialist in mental disorders): A retouched calotype portrait by Henry Collen. (Science Museum,
London)

Figure 11. Lord Langdale, 1829: A miniature painting by
Henry Collen. Collen, who was the first professional calo-
type photographer, was also miniature painter to Queen
Victoria. (Science Museum, London)

Figure 12. Daguerreotype portraits by T. R. Williams from a stereo pair: A gentleman and a lady, 2¾″ × 2¼″. (Science Museum, London)

Antoine Claudet was a great admirer of Talbot and initially introduced the calotype into his studio at the Adelaide Gallery with enthusiasm. He wrote to Talbot:

> I spare no expense or trouble to make it a success. I would be ashamed if anyone could accuse me of the contrary. Until we have a paper with a surface as uniform and perfect as a silver plate I say that the Daguerreotype gives images more delicate, finer and of greater perfection than the Talbotype. Until we can operate with the Talbotype in several seconds and as rapidly with as the Daguerreotype, so that one can get more pleasing poses, then I say that the advantage is on the side of the Daguerreotype. But I also say that the Talbotype has beauty which the other has not, that the impressions are more portable and circulate more easily, that it is possible to send them through the post, stick them in albums, etc., and finally, one can obtain an unlimited number of copies.[29]

Claudet struggled to make the calotype popular at the Adelaide but with very little encouragement from the public, who seemed to prefer the retouched daguerreotype to the more "impressionistic" calotype. Profits fell and within a few years of his initial enthusiasm, Claudet returned to the daguerreotype for portraits.

Talbot's assumptions about the potential of the calotype for interpretive portraiture were realized by David Octavius Hill, a Scottish portrait painter from Perth. Hill's calotypes represent the final stage in a tradition of portraiture, which had dominated British painting in the eighteenth century, and continued to do so into the nineteenth. Perhaps Hill's special talent was sparked by the rich period of cultural activity in which he worked, a period that included the birth of photography and the rebirth of Scottish portrait painting, with the advent of Henry Raeburn and his sucessors John Gordon and John Gilbert. (Or it may have been that Hill's relationship with his partner Robert Adamson provided a magic combination of scientific and artistic skills.) For whatever reason, the pair produced portraits of a quality yet to be surpassed in photography.

In 1843, two years after Talbot published his invention, Hill was commissioned to paint a portrait of the First General Assembly of the newly formed Free Church of Scotland. Hill had been experimenting with calotypy, and since the painting required 470 individual portraits, he resolved to use photographs of his sitters as models. For the next five years Hill, with Adamson, photographed subjects from every level of society, at Rocks House,

Figure 13. "Reverend Dr. Burns." Calotype. (Metropolitan Museum of Art, Harris Brisbane Dick Fund, N.Y.)

Figure 14. (*opposite*) Newhaven fishwives. Calotype. (Metropolitan Museum of Art, Harris Brisbane Dick Fund, N.Y.)

Figure 15. Newhaven fisherman and three boys. Calotype. (Metropolitan Museum of Art, Harris Brisbane Dick Fund, N.Y.)

Figure 16. "Cookie Miller." Calotype. (Metropolitan Museum of Art, Harris Brisbane Dick Fund, N.Y.)

their studio at the foot of Carlton Hill in Edinburgh. Their subjects included the painters William Etty, Francis Grant, and John Everett Millais, Adam Smith, Robert Burns, William Robertson (the historian), Sir Walter Scott, and many others. They also portrayed members of the Scottish working class, fisherwomen, street people, urchins, friends, and family, with the same sophisticated handling of the camera. Hill had the vision of both a painter and a photographer: he was able to extract from his surroundings exciting compositional arrangements of shape and form, and at the same time recognize the poignancy of a fleeting moment.

Hill and Adamson's portraits depend for their expression on a quality we now term "photographic"—the configuration of graphic tones. To compensate for the slow speed of the calotype lens, most portraits were taken out of doors, and Hill repeatedly demonstrated his understanding of the special properties of sunlight by manipulating subtle transitions from bright luminous patches to rich deep tones. In his portrait of The Reverend Dr. Burns (Figure 13), for example, Hill uses the light falling on the forehead and the side of the face toward the camera to catch all the essential details of the face without destroying a sense of intimacy with harsh overall lighting. The highlights emphasize skin texture, flesh lines, the texture of his lips and jowls—realistic detail—while the shadows protect the personal mystery of the man. The man's pose, with his hands clasped, thumbs barely touching, is curiously real.

The series of portraits Hill and Adamson made of local fishermen and women concern the lives and lifestyle of the people of Newhaven. Hill, with his painter's training, exploited the visually rich traditions of the fishing village, so that the portraits can be viewed as ethnographic studies, or as art work, or both. In one group portrait (Figure 14), Hill counterpoints the rough material and striped pattern of the native costume with the smooth curved shapes of the fishing baskets. A head tilts downward, a hand is placed with fingers resting horizontally across the round basket; the image arrests the eye, not only for subjective reasons, but by the interplay of shapes and forms. In another from the Newhaven series, a man leans on a boat with three young boys at his feet (Figure 15). The angle at the front of the boat is repeated by the angle of the man's elbow at the right of the picture, and the figures of the boys provide the necessary compositional balance to the strong image above. The picture was not the result of chance; examination of Hill and Adamson's work shows they tried many similar compositions, but the picture preserves a sense of naturalness, and the Newhaven series stands as a moving record of folk life in a Scottish fishing village.

Hill was extremely observant of human characteristics—particularly of nuances of gesture and manner that were peculiar to his subjects. The portrait of Cookie Miller (Figure 16) is an example: the sitter is posed, hand on stick, mouth on the brink of a smile, as if glimpsed in a special, private moment. Subtle changes in body position, a shift in sunlight, the addition of a personal prop, were all essential details to Hill. Though this is not unusual among modern photographers, it should be remembered that Hill had no predecessors—no established methods and no traditions other than those of nineteenth century painting to guide him.

The contribution of Robert Adamson to the work of D. O Hill should not be minimized. Adamson has been allotted the technician's role by most historians and critics, but it is more probable that he was essential to the creative process, exchanging ideas with Hill and helping to realize the final image. Hill's dependence on Adamson becomes evident when we consider that Hill was active in photography only from 1843 until Adamson's death in January, 1848.

After Adamson's death, Hill, who had accumulated a large amount of material for his painting, returned to his original occupation—a mediocre artist, producing forgettable pictures. The calotype portraits he and Adamson produced were remarkable as pictures, but perhaps most interesting as indicators of the road future photographers might travel and the heights they might attain.

Notes

1. Helmut and Alison Gernsheim, *The History of Photography,* McGraw-Hill, N.Y. 1969, p. 69.

2. *Ibid.* The special commission was set up to decide the value of the daguerreotype to France, and would advise the French government to purchase exclusive rights to the invention.

3. Niépce found that when a pewter surface was coated with bitumen of Judea, a light-sensitive substance, and exposed to light for upwards of eight hours, a positive picture resulted. Through a freak accident, Daguerre discovered that a latent image could be brought out with mercury vapor, reducing exposure time to twenty minutes (approximately). In May, 1837, he discovered he could fix the image for permanence with a solution of salt.

4. *Athenaeum,* October 26, 1839, p. 813.

5. *The Art-Union,* April 1842, p. 82.

6. Litigation involving Daguerre and other patentees continued inconclusively until the expiration of the original patent in 1853. By that time, owing to newer technical developments, the daguerreotype process was little used.

7. Francis S. Beatty, *Year-Book of Photography and Photographic News Almanac,* 1864, p. 77.

8. Arthur Gill, "J. F. Goddard and the Daguerreotype Process," Part I, *Photographic Journal,* November 1966, p. 371.

9. "Daguerreotype Portraits," *The Morning Chronicle,* September 12, 1840, col. 2.

10. *The Spectator,* March, 1841, p. 283.

11. *Photographic News,* August 8, 1879.

12. *British Journal of Photography,* October 30, 1868, p. 521.

13. *British Journal of Photography,* January 3, 1868, p. 4.

14. *Illustrated London News,* June 15, 1844.

15. *The Spectator,* 1841, p. 861.

16. *Ibid.,* 1841, pp. 860-861.

17. *Ibid.*

18. *The Art-Journal,* December 12, 1840, No. 23.

19. Thomas Sutton, "Reminiscences of an Old Photographer," *British Journal of Photography,* August 30, 1867.

20. Robert Taft, *Photography and the American Scene,* Dover, N.Y. 1938, p. 78.

21. *Science Museum Photography Catalogue,* Science Museum, London, p. 49.

22. *Ibid.,* pp. 26-27.

23. *Athenaeum,* February 9, 1839, p. 115.

24. D. B. Thomas, *The First Negatives,* Science Museum Monograph, London, 1964, p. 9.

25. William Henry Fox Talbot, *The Pencil of Nature,* June, 1844, Section XIV, "The Ladder."

26. M. T. Talbot, "The Life and Personality of Fox Talbot," *Journal Of The Royal Society of Arts,* p. 830.

27. *The Art-Union,* May, 1845, p. 138.

28. Beaumont Newhall, *The History of Photography,* Museum of Modern Art, George Eastman House, Rochester. Quoted in a letter from D. O. Hill to Mr. Bicknell, January 17, 1848, Coll. GEH, Rochester, N.Y.

29. Quoted in D. B. Thomas, *op. cit.,* p. 28.

2

Photography and
the Victorian Psyche

For the early Victorians, the experience of being photographed involved much more than the sitter's vanity. In much the same way as the Dutch put on their walls paintings of elaborate meals, with dishes laden with food, in order to create the impression of wealth in the home, the Victorians kept likenesses of themselves. The impression they hoped to convey had less to do with wealth than with social position and rank, and more especially with moral character. The photographer, still coping with technical difficulties, was given the arduous task of combining, in each portrait, a testimonial to the sitter's status in society with the traits valued in the character of the individual. It was a time when people were concerned far more with their image in the eyes of their contemporaries than with the idea of mankind, with being part of the human race. A portrait photograph served the utilitarian function of helping to maintain the social order—the Victorians intended that others who were less fortunate might benefit from their example and that future generations would model themselves after the social ideal shown in the photographs.

The Victorian ideal was a traditional beauty closely linked to dignity, propriety and seriousness of purpose. By the middle of the century, preoccupation with standards of propriety became particularly characteristic of Victorian lifestyle, and was connected with a new awareness—particularly a

33

new class consciousness—that was reflected in the portraits of the period. John Harrison, a historian writing about the period, explains:

> The middle class (perhaps more than the working classes) were class conscious . . .contemporary writers refer time and again to the same criteria: occupation, types of expenditure, and pattern of family living. As the middle classes opposed aristocratic idleness and excess with their puritan values of hard work and sobriety, or held themselves up as a model to the labouring poor and preached to them the doctrine of Malthus, they constantly reminded themselves of their distinctive position. . . .[1]

Harrison's explanation makes it clear that the Victorians deliberately culti-vated this image themselves. Henry James, remarking in *The Portrait of A Lady,* of the Misses Molyneux—that "there were fifty thousand young women in England who exactly resembled them"[2]—touches an essential aspect of the Victorian period: Uniformity of appearance and a standard code of behavior strengthened class distinction and served to solidify middle class values and mores.

The Victorians exercised prudent restraint in matters of appearance, and this influenced the popular concept of "beauty." Although the Victorians were as conscious as we are today of presenting an attractive facade, the attri-butes to be displayed in a portrait photograph were, foremost, the qualities of a gentleman or gentlewoman—breeding shown by understatement and dignity. Dorothea Brooke, the heroine of Eliot's *Middlemarch* embodies the ideal:

> . . . she had the kind of beauty that seemed to be thrown into relief by poor dress . . . her profile as well as her stature and bearing seemed to gain the more dignity from her plain garments. . . Miss Brooke's plain dressing was due to mixed conditions, in most of which her sister shared. The pride of being ladies had something to do with it: the Brooke connections, though not exactly aristocratic were unquestionably 'good': if you enquired backward for a generation or two you would not find any yard-measuring or parcel-tying forefathers. . . . Young women of such birth naturally regarded frippery as the ambition of a huckster's daughter.[3]

The English middle class gentleperson was one who had confidence enough in birthright superiority not to have to flaunt his position ostentatiously. Mrs. Gaskell portrays the same ideal in Margaret, the heroine of *North and South*:

> . . . a young lady came forward with frank dignity—a young lady of a
> different type to most that he was in the habit of seeing [in industrial
> Milton]. Her dress was very plain: a close straw bonnet of the best material
> and shape, trimmed with white ribbon; a dark silk gown, without any
> trimming or flounce; a large Indian shawl, which hung about her in long
> heavy folds, and which she wore as an Empress wears her drapery. He did
> not understand who she was, as he caught the simple, straight, unabashed
> look, which showed that his being there was of no concern to the beautiful
> countenance, and called up no flush of surprise to the pale ivory of the
> complexion . . . her full beauty met his eye; her round, white, flexile throat
> rising out of the full yet lithe figure; her lips moving so slightly as she
> spoke, not breaking the cold serene look of her face with any variation
> from the one lovely, haughty curve; her eyes with their soft gloom,
> meeting his with quiet, maiden freedom . . .[4]

Mrs. Gaskell emphasizes that the sensuality and physical beauty of this woman
is heightened by her plain clothes and straightforward, modest behavior.
Although the narrator knows nothing about her, he senses that she is
"different" from the nouveau-riche inhabitants of the industrial northern
town, because she has the self-confidence of being well-bred which makes
elaborate costume or ostentatious behavior unnecessary. The narrator, who is
a man, also acknowledges that she is virginal, an essential aspect of the model
Victorian gentlewoman, because she seems unaware of his intense scrutiny,
even when they meet eye to eye, and unconcerned with her physical beauty.
Modesty, chastity, dignity, and pride are all aspects of beauty in Victorian
terms, as much as facial features and figure.

Contrast the descriptions of Margaret and Dorothea with the portrait of the
villainess in *Middlemarch,* Rosamond Vincy. Rosamond (whose grandfather was
an innkeeper) is conscious of both her physical beauty and the impression she
makes on men:

> . . . Every nerve and muscle in Rosamond was adjusted to the consciousness
> that she was being looked at. She was by nature an actress of parts that
> entered into her physique; she even acted her own character and so well
> that she did not know it to be completely her own. . .[5]

Eliot purposely chooses phrases which emphasized the flirtatious and artificial
character of Rosamond: she "dimples," scrutinizes herself in the mirror, and
gloats to her plainer friend (who is incidently another model Victorian

gentlewoman) over the difference in their physical charms. Eliot attributes to her none of the subtleties of taste or bearing that we find in Dorothea Brooke; Rosamond's refinements have all been carefully studied:

> . . . Rosamond Vincy who had excellent taste in costume, with that nymph-like figure and pure blondness which gave the largest range to choice in the flow and colour of drapery. But these things made only part of her charm. She was admitted to be the flower of Mrs. Lemon's school, the chief school in the county, where the teaching included all that was demanded in the accomplished female—even to the extras, such as the getting in and out of a carriage.[6]

The Victorian reader would be alerted by certain clues, for example, the suggestion of elaborate styles and colorful clothes, and the ability to be aware of a man's admiration without blushing, that Rosamond's character was less than noble. Rosamond's virtues are vulgar because they are not modified or subtle, and her charms are the product of training, not heritage. Lacking the restraint and dignity of the ideal Victorian lady, the reader knows she was bound to make her husband miserable, and come to an unpleasant end as opposed to Miss Brooke and Margaret, whose quiet yet courageous, proud yet modest, beautiful yet dignified countenances predict that they will remain loyal to husband and home.

Victorian men were also conscious of the impression they made on others. Uniformity in men's clothing began with Beau Brummel, who insisted that a gentleman could wear nothing other than a plain blue coat. This brought about the fashion for somber, anonymous costume, affected by men of the period as being expressive of their seriousness and solidarity of purpose. Victorian men also presented a shield to the world by adhering to a rigid code of behavior, so that the disguise of being a gentleman (and that included supressing physical desire and emotion) served almost as a protection from the real world in which they lived.

Portrait photography became yet another method to promote the ideal and to shield from the lower classes, and from posterity, any character flaws which might exist. To this day, we imagine the Victorians as they appeared in their photographs—upright, somberly dressed, puritanical—and when we learn from their diaries or private journals of secret sexual desires, liaisons, or forbidden practices, we find them hard to reconcile with the physical picture we have of the individual. The historian C. Willett Cunnington describes the Victorian inclination toward disguise this way:

When we refer to the "Victorian Gothic" period, it is to the 40's that we turn to find the most typical examples, and not merely in architecture and furniture design; the notion that reality could and should be disguised by forms serving no other purpose than as a veil over ugly Truth, was the essence of it. It explained the desire to make a railway station resemble a church (which was not only prettier but more moral); supplied an air of holiness to the dining-room furniture, and transformed a mere picture into a lesson. It inspired Ruskin to demand that factories should be made as unlike factories as possible, and Pugin to see that true Faith could be expressed only by a pointed arch. But it also explained the novelist's careful distortion of facts, so that Dickens could draw the character of Nancy without mentioning the essential fact that she was a prostitute, and Charlotte Bronte could draw a bedroom scene without a bed.[7]

Unquestionably, Victorian preference was for a species of "realism" that reflected the attitudes and prejudices of the period, and with this in mind, we can better understand the uneasiness with which the first sitters greeted the photographic medium, which was publicized as a "mirror of nature." Herbert Fry, who attempted in the mid-fifties to form a National Gallery of Photographic Portraits,[8] found himself faced with resistance—indicative of the Victorians' need to control any medium with the potential to penetrate the social structure. Although sixteen parts of the "National Gallery" were eventually published, Fry received many refusals, some expressing carefully worded protests against the intrusive powers of photography, and some showing concern about the resulting photograph, which did not present the sitter as he wished to be seen. Lord Palmerston wrote that his wife thought the likenesses very bad, and she advised Palmerston (with an eye to the history books, perhaps) that he ought not to have them published (Figure 17). Lord Lyndhurst, Lord High Chancellor of Great Britain, wrote to Fry requesting that his portrait be withdrawn (Figure 18): "All my friends and acquaintances think that your photographic portrait is such an abominable caricature that I must request you to cancel it and substitute a more believable specimen in its place."[9] Undoubtedly a more "believable specimen" would show the façade of the statesman as he wished to be remembered and fewer flaws of the human being. In both cases, the sitters attempted to control the photographer—by the end of the fifties the professional photographer would learn to shoot with his sitter's expectations in mind.

Other candidates for Fry's gallery indicated that photography had negative associations of a social character that made it undesirable for them to pose. The

Figure 17. Henry John Temple, 3rd Viscount Palmerston, March 30, 1857, 188 × 154 mm. (oval) by Herbert Watkins.

Figure 18. John Singleton Copley, Baron Lyndhurst, April 8, 1857,
206 × 154 mm. (oval), by Herbert Watkins.

Figure 19. Professor Francis William Newman, c. 1857, 190 × 150 mm. (oval) by Herbert Watkins for Fry's gallery.

Figure 20. Philip Henry Stanhope, 5th Earl of Stanhope, March 7, 1857, 187 × 153 mm. (oval) by Herbert Watkins.

novelist Elizabeth Gaskell replied to Fry's request as if she had been asked to perform an act of indecency: "Other women may not object to having their portrait taken for the public and sold indiscriminately but I feel a strong insurmountable object to it . . . ."[10] Mrs. Gaskell, who is the subject of many drawings and painted portraits (Figure 21), must have found the democratic nature of the new medium to be particularly demeaning. She recognized one of the most significant aspects of portrait photography—that everybody, regard-

". . . Other women may not object to having their portraits taken for the public and sold indiscriminately, but I feel a strong insurmountable objection to it."

Figure 21. Elizabeth Gaskell, chalk drawing by G. Richmond, 1851. (National Portrait Gallery, London)

less of name or class, had access to a photographer's studio. Photography, in the words of one commentator, had:

> . . . swept away many of the illiberal distinctions of rank and wealth, so that the poor man, who possesses but a few shillings, can command as lifelike a portrait of his wife or child as Sir Thomas Lawrence painted for the most distinguished sovereigns of Europe . . .[11]

Mrs. Gaskell was not alone in recognizing the dangerous potential that portrait photography had for weakening the societal boundaries that had been so carefully established. Over the next decade the style for society portraiture

"Novels and plays had to be such as father could read aloud to his wife and daughters without embarrassment . . ."

—John Harrison from
The Early Victorians

Figure 22. Dickens reading to his daughters (after a photograph). (National Portrait Gallery, London)

would become more exactly defined, so that portrait photography became one more tool for clarifying distinctions of rank and class.

Some objected to portrait photography for exactly the reason it became popular—while the camera could reveal all the details of the outer aspects of a person, they felt that it was unable to penetrate any of the inner aspects, the amalgamation of experiences that balance each other and combine to produce personality within the unique being. Balzac disliked photography for this reason as he told Nadar, the famous French photographer:

> I am composed of a multitude of spectra which intersperse my body in a great number of layers. Your plates will never be able to catch these spectra which form my essential self, but can only record some pose of my body.[12]

An early writer on photography, Charles Pearce, touches on the problem in an article in which he maintains that neither good or bad looks influence people in regard to being photographed, but that the people who enjoy being photographed are those whose "expressions never vary by a hair's-breadth from their dead level of satisfied uniformity."[13] As Pearce notes, Oliver Wendell Holmes explained the problem this way: he saw at least six personalities distinctly to be recognized as taking part in a dialogue—say, between John and Thomas:

THREE JOHNS
1   The real John, known only to his Maker
2   John's ideal John; never the real one and often unlike him
3   Thomas's ideal John; never the real John, nor John's John, but a John very unlike either

THREE THOMASES
1   The real Thomas
2   Thomas's ideal Thomas
3   John's ideal Thomas

According to Holmes, John's dislike of being photographed arises from his fear that the portrait may not be like the ideal John. If he attempts to get the picture of his ideal it will most assuredly be condemned by Thomas.[14] Pearce adds his own conclusion, that it is this principle of multiple personality through which the objections of people who do not wish to be photographed arise. They do not care to be exposed to the risk of being represented by a picture which is certainly not their ideal, and they are not aware that this "unlike" portrait may in reality represent them perfectly in the eyes of their friends.[15]

Many Victorians voiced adamant protest against the invasion of privacy resulting from having their portrait photograph taken. There are numerous court cases against photographers who exhibited portraits without consent of the sitter. A Mr. Brooks, a photographer in Oxford Street, brought his neighbor to court for destroying two portraits exhibited in his showcase as specimens.[16] His neighbor defended himself on the grounds that the photographer had no right to use these likenesses, which were portraits of his wife, without her permission. The neighbor faced a problem that has yet to be resolved about the degree to which the photographer and the subject have possession of the final portrait. The photographer, who had made the image, conceivably wanted to display his work and his talent to the public. The sitter's husband saw the portrait as bearing a direct connection to the personality of his wife, and felt he should, as legal guardian of his wife, be able to control her photographic portrait as well. John Ruskin voiced similar resentment when he replied to Fry's request that he sit for his portrait photograph. His rudeness reveals, if not direct anxiety, at least resentment at the photographer's apparent attempt to manipulate him:

> I dislike grammar—and I don't know much about it—but I know the difference between an indicative and a conditional and expect my correspondents to do the same. My letter contained no promise to you whatsoever but merely the statement that I *may* not *will* agree to your proposal after enquiries are made.[17]

I believe that many Victorians felt the photographer had a power over them: he and his arts were beyond their control. A good deal of this fear came from not understanding the mechanics of the process, but fear of portraits in general dates back centuries and has been reported in England in relatively recent times. James Napier wrote of people in the west of Scotland "who refuse to have likenesses taken lest it prove unlucky; and gave as instances the cases of several of their friends who never had a day's health after being photographed."[18] P. H. Groome recorded the following in 1888, in a study of gypsy life:

> An artist once vainly attempted to sketch a gypsy girl. "I won't have her drawed out," said the girl's aunt. "I told her I'd make her scrawl the earth

before me, if she ever let herself be drawed out again." "Why what harm can there be?" "I know there's a fiz [a charm] in it. There was my youngest, that the gorja drawed out on Newmarket Heath, she never held her head up after, but wasted away and died, and she's buried in March churchyard."[19]

One of the impressions that pervade the correspondence Fry received is the need for self-protection, the need to defend oneself from the photographer and the public. Professor Francis Newman of University College writes:

> To have error in dry facts is disagreeable enough (and is always to be apprehended when the writer is not a near friend and in connection with one's kinsfolk and other personal friends), and to have a stupid reproduction would be worst of all. It is time enough to write memoirs of private men, I think, after they are dead and I cannot encourage what would be to me simply annoying.[20]

Alfred Lord Tennyson wrote that he hated being taken at all and had denied similar requests to friends.[21] In these and other cases the prospective sitters indicate a strong need for their privacy to be respected; one suspects also a hint of superstitious feeling, the unacknowledged fear that they (like the gypsy girl) could be in some way endangered by having their portraits taken. Belief in the magical power of "likenesses" is, of course, widespread in primitive cultures, and fear of the camera has often been reported. Villagers in Sikhim, for example, hid away whenever the lens of the camera, or "the evil eye of the box," was pointed at them, because they thought it took away their souls. The owner of the camera also had the power, so they thought, to cast spells on them.[22] When Joseph Thomson attempted to photograph some of the Wa-teita in Eastern Africa, they imagined that he was a magician trying to obtain possession of their souls and that if he got their likenesses they themselves would be at his mercy.[23]

Such eminent and sophisticated Victorians as Alfred Lord Tennyson or Professor Newman were hardly harboring superstitious beliefs of this sort. It is possible, however, that the fear and suspicion found in these primitive tribes concerning the "capture" of a person's likeness may be based on a subconscious belief of a fundamental and possibly universal character. It should be noted, too, that for all its advances in science and technology, the Victorian era was permeated with superstition and supernatural beliefs—a period when people were susceptible to almost any kind of religious or magical propaganda. The "magical" element should certainly not be overlooked as a factor preying on the sitter's imagination.[24]

In a short story titled *The Photograph*, Nigel Kneale suggests the extent to which Victorians may have ascribed extraordinary powers to the portrait and portrait photographer. Kneale relates the tale of a mother who takes her dying son, not to a priest or a doctor, but to a photographer. The boy realises that he is dying when he is photographed, and does indeed die. He believes that once his image is recorded in the photograph, there is no longer a need for his body to remain alive, because the portrait photograph has become the house for his soul: "Tears came out of his eyes. He felt angry and frightened; as if he had lost part of himself."[25] The reader is left to ponder the real reason for the little boy's death—was it his illness, exposure to the cold on the way to the photographer's studio, or was it the magical powers of the camera, and the photographer who said: "Keep still. Keep-quite-quite-quite-still!"?

The mother who wanted to have her dying son's photograph taken—and who risked shortening his life still further to have it done—was following a practice common to this time: "Kindly remember, Doctor, I am the child's mother," she says. "I wanted this memory of him to keep. More than anything you could understand."[26] The portrait photograph is more to her than merely a remembrance or keepsake. She seems to regard the photograph as the house for her little boy's soul—or at least as a surviving part of him. Although exaggerated for melodramatic effect, Kneale's story gives an accurate sense of the connection the Victorians made between photographic portraiture and superstitious beliefs, especially those surrounding death.

That the Victorians attached great importance to the photographic portrait is evidenced by the lengths they went to in preserving portraits of family members after death. Funeral albums were often inset with clocks at the top of the cover, set to the time of the death of a loved one whose portrait was included in the album, and often these albums amounted to nothing less than shrines for the dead. Public demand for funeral portraits, taken after death, grew enormously in the first three decades after the introduction of the photograph.[27] Many families, like the Spencers of Leicester, kept a family history in album form of their children alive and dead—a somewhat macabre photographic record in many instances (Figures 23 and 24). The photographs were usually tinted, taken of the children dressed in their best clothing, often only a few weeks before they died. Also included, sometimes as a frontispiece to the album, were photographs of their graves.

Funeral photographs tended to be a record of the person as the family wanted him to be remembered, a final step in assuring that posterity would retain an edifying image of the deceased. The Kodak Museum outside London has an example of a portrait of a dead child photographed in its coffin, which served as a testimonial to the affluence of the family (Figure 25). The elaborate oval gold frame bound in velvet and leather, the white lace dress of the child, the tinted flowers, and the mahogany coffin, photographed from an angle allowing the intricate gold handles to be seen to the best advantage—all are given more importance in the picture than the face of the child. The funeral portrait served to show the family's status and wealth as much as it served as a remembrance. The attention drawn to the coffin and the accessories of the death ceremony in such photographs are reminiscent of the Egyptian preparation for a prosperous afterlife.[28] The Egyptians ensured comfort for their dead in the afterlife by burying their possessions with them; the Victorians, if they could not take it with them, at least had the portrait photograph as evidence of the achievements, both economic and social, of the deceased and the family at the time of death.

The Victorians were themselves image-makers for pragmatic reasons that had social implications reaching beyond the whims of fashion. Perhaps more than modern sitters, who take photography very much for granted, the Victorians suffered from the fear of appearing foolish, or ugly, or both, in the camera's eye. The mistaken notion that the camera actually records "reality" was taken to mean that an ugly photograph must be truthful, even if the sitter was usually regarded as attractive. Portrait photographs were often rejected as unsatisfactory because the images were both too literal, allowing little room for imagination or association, and too "fixed" or static in expression. *Photographic News* relates this incident:

> A lady sat for a portrait in the absence of the principal. The lady was fastidious, and the operator was patient. In turn, every possible view of the face had been tried; right-side, left-side, front, three-quarters, and profile, and almost every modification between; but the lady was dissatisfied and she resolved to try again the next day when the principal would be home. Presenting herself next morning and explaining the case she was blandly received by M. M— who had heard all the particulars. "Be so good as to take a seat here madam," placing a chair with its back to the camera. The lady, wondering, did as she was desired; Mr. M— then proceeded gravely to place the headrest to the forehead instead of as usual to the back of the

Florence Ann Spencer, Died Oct. 16, 1865, Aged 4 Yrs.

Dépose

Figure 24. Florence Spencer, from the family
funeral album, 1865. (Kodak Museum,
Harrow and Wealdstone)

Figure 23. (*opposite*). Spencer family funeral album.
(Kodak Museum, Harrow and Wealdstone)

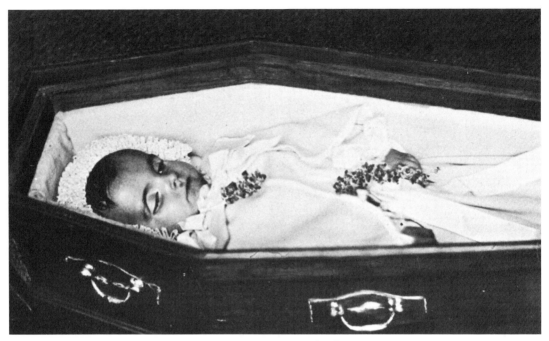

Figure 25. Collodion positive (ambrotype) death portrait, 1856. (Kodak Museum, Harrow and Wealdstone)

head. Having focussed, and put the plate in the camera, he said, "Now madam, if you will be so good as to remain quite still for a few moments. . ." "Why Mr.—, you are about to take the back of my head!" exclaimed the lady. "Precisely so, madam. That is the only change now left to us. I have the pictures taken and they are all excellent Daguerreotypes, and very good likenesses. Every possible view of the face has been tried, our only chance of pleasing now is by trying a portrait in which the face will be entirely absent."[29]

Obviously this lady did not have the same picture of herself in her mind as the one conceived by the photographer. One reason for this was the same reason we often do not see ourselves as others see us—we are inclined to see aspects of ourselves when we look in the mirror, rather than the whole of the face at once. In this case, the photographer's camera recorded other aspects than those she saw in herself, and the result alarmed her.

Memory also plays a part in coloring our imagination. If we become excited at hearing the footsteps of someone we love, the association with our past experience with that person excites us, rather than the footsteps. In much the same way, when we view a portrait, the emotions we feel about the subject spring from associations we have with a particular expression or pose, not from the actual portrait. The lady in this incident was unable to find a connection between her past experiences, what she imagined about herself, and the portraits taken by the photographer. Instead she saw immobile features, unrelieved by the play of expression which gives the face its charm and which triggers the memory to associate the image with past events, and so she complained that the photographs were not successful likenesses. Many of the complaints Fry received from sitters for his photographic gallery probably stemmed from the same source, because the Victorians had not become accustomed, as we have, to seeing their mirror image translated into a graphic portrait that captures only the particular moment.

Of course, this lady hoped to be flattered. Her idea of herself was most likely molded by compliments she had received and by Victorian tastes, which were very carefully defined. The Victorians suffered, as we do today, from over-exposure to a standard conception of what was beautiful. The Victorian equivalent to, say, the Vogue cover girl was exemplified in various ladies' magazines, and popular novels repeatedly praised a particular style of good-looking heroines. This was the ideal for beauty in Victorian woman:

> . . . dark, silken hair braided back over a small, well-developed head; her forehead lofty, and full and open . . . the eyebrows perfect in arch and form; the eyes round, soft or flashing . . . grey, well-formed and beautifully set—the lashes long and black, the under ones turning down with a delicate curve, and forming a soft relief upon the tint of her cheek, which, when she enjoyed good health, was bright and blushing. Her complexion was delicately fair, her skin soft and transparent, her nose small (retroussé), the nostril well-defined, slightly curved but capable of a scornful expression . . . her mouth . . . was neither flat nor pouting, neither large nor small, the under jaw projected a little beyond the upper, her smile was deliciously animated; her teeth white, small and even, and her voice and laugh, soft, low and musical; her ears were of peculiar beauty . . . very small and of a

Figure 26. Portrait of a lady, ambrotype, 66 × 52 mm.
(Victoria and Albert Museum, London)

delicate hue, and her hands and feet even smaller than her sylph-like figure
would have led one to expect.[30]

The lady in question probably defined her good and bad points in terms of a
standard of beauty very similar to that expressed above. She may have been
proud of her fair complexion or her pouting mouth, but although these details
were presumably revealed in the daguerreotype photograph, they assumed
equal, not greater, importance in the image with all the other less perfect
details of her face.

The incident illustrates one essential difficulty with portrait photography—

that the portrait, reflecting a multi-faceted human being, must be realized in a moment, and once realized remains fixed and unchangeable. The problem becomes more complex when the photographer's aim and the sitter's desire go beyond recording facial features to a more penetrating portrait of the individual. The quality of the portrait photograph is determined by the photographer's ability to coordinate what he senses about the individual posing for him with his own perception of the complete picture of human life.

By the mid-fifties, photography was well launched as a business, and the art of photographic portraiture refined to a point. The Victorian years saw the emergence of two separate, strongly motivated groups of photographers—the commercial portraitists who were concerned with the public, and others whose concerns were private and subjective. It would be safe to say that very little communication existed between the two groups, and the public, for the most part, paid little attention to the non-commercial photographer. Since the commercial photographer represented the Victorian sitters as they wanted to be remembered, and their less commercial comrades recorded a personal impression of each sitter, we are left with a collection of elegant half-truths—how deceptive is a portrait medium which gives the impression of recording physical reality! The viewer has the difficult task of untangling realities—penetrating the facade of the sitter and the prejudices of the photographer, for insight into the Victorian consciousness.

Notes

1. J. F. C. Harrison, *The Early Victorians 1832–51*, Panther Books Ltd., London 1973, pp. 104 ff. Harrison lists three basics to middle class life in Victorian England: (1) an income above £300 ($600) annually; (2) a particular occupation or calling; (3) the proper education, religious affiliation, and style of home. In addition he mentions a house of suitable size and location, furnishings, food, dress, carriages, and domestic service.

The lower middle classes were small manufacturers, shopkeepers, coal and corn merchants, master tailors, inn keepers, commercial dealers, tradesmen, clerks, office workers, and school teachers—respectable people who did not have to live by manual labor. The haute bourgeoisie lived on familiar terms with and intermarried with aristocracy. They included London bankers, city merchants, industrial magnates, and anyone who could become wealthy and gain respect.

2. Henry James, *The Portrait of a Lady*, Penguin Books Ltd., Middlesex, England, 1973, p. 75.

3. George Eliot, *Middlemarch*, New American Library, N.Y. 1964, pp. 9 ff.

4. Elizabeth Gaskell, *North and South,* Penguin, London, 1970, p. 99.

5. George Eliot, *op. cit.,* p. 117.

6. *Ibid.,* p. 96.

7. C. Willett Cunnington, *Feminine Attitudes in the Nineteenth Century,* London, 1955, p. 106.

8. Herbert Fry, collection comprising about 139 letters addressed to Fry by various eminent Victorians with a view to including them in one or other of his publications, National Portrait Gallery Photographic Collection.

9. *Ibid.*

10. *Ibid.*

11. *Photographic News,* London, 1861.

12. Alex Strasser, *Immortal Portraits,* London, 1848, p. 22.

13. Charles Pearce, *Year-Book of Photography and Photographic News Annual,* London, 1887, pp. 49–51.

14. Oliver Wendell Holmes, *The Autocrat of the Breakfast Table,* London, J. M. Dent & Sons, Ltd., 1960, p. 51.

15. Charles Pearce, *op. cit.*

16. *Photographic News,* April 8, 1859, pp. 49–50.

17. Fry's collection of letters, *op. cit.*

18. James Napier, *Folk-Lore or Superstitious Beliefs in the West of Scotland,* pp. 142 ff.

19. From F. H. Groome, *In Gypsy Tents,* Edinburgh, 1880, pp. 337 ff., as cited by James George Frazer, *The Golden Bough: A Study in Magic and Religion,* London: Macmillan & Co. Ltd., 1951.

20. Fry's collection of letters, *op. cit.*

21. *Ibid.*

22. From L. A. Waddell, *Among the Himalayans,* Westminster, 1889, pp. 85 ff. as cited in Frazer, *op. cit.,* Part 2.

23. From J. Thompson, *Through Masai Land,* London, 1885, p. 86 sq., as cited by Frazer, *op. cit.,* Part 2.

24. Frazer writes that fear of the portrait existed throughout the 19th century in Europe. In an article in *Blackwoods Magazine* written in February 1886 he mentions that some old women in the Greek Isles were very angry at having their likenesses drawn, thinking that in consequence they would pine and die. The German superstition that if you have your portrait painted you will die is discussed by J. A. E. Kohler, in *Volksbranch, Aberglauben, Sagen und Ander Alte Uberlieferungen im Voigtlande,* Leipzig, 1867, p. 423.

25. Nigel Kneale, *Tomato Cain and Other Stories,* Collins Press, London, 1919, p. 129.

26. *Ibid.*

27. The annual reports of the Registrar General for England and Wales showed that between 1839 and 1851 the annual number of deaths of infants under one year was usually between 150 and 160 per 1,000 live births. In the late forties, the death rate for infants, as for the whole population, rose appreciably. All of

which meant that the ordinary Victorian family was intimately acquainted with death in a way that is rare today. To insure two surviving children, a married couple could expect to have five or six births.

28. The Egyptians believed in a kind of material persistence after death. It is evident that the deceased was thought to pass a ghostly existence, in the form of KA—sometimes called the double—in the actual tomb chamber. Most of the arts of Pharonic Egypt, especially the portrait statues which could be infused with the spirit of the deceased, owed their origin to this belief. To guard against the destruction of the embalmed body, the idea was fostered that a properly constructed and sanctified image, usually a portrait outlined upon the wall, would satisfy the disembodied spirit. Wall paintings on colored relief, of possessions, were also part of the tomb chamber.

29. *Photographic News,* August 16, 1861, p. 383.

30. *The Art-Union,* February 15, 1839, "Portraits of L. E. L.," p. 3.

lea
tal
un
ca
sai
re:
lik
pa
ex
an

which have not been preserved in one body, the viewer must serve the critic's function and distinguish between the significant part of a photographer's work and other images produced as a result of experimentation.)

Claudet seems to have been at war with his instincts as he became more successful as a portrait photographer. Probably more than other daguerreotypists, Claudet had a passionate interest in the science of photography and throughout his career he experimented with the many aspects of what the camera could do.* Among a body of rather dull, imitation miniature paintings, there are some portraits that reveal an exciting sense of personal involvement with his subjects, expressed in photographic terms. The imitation miniatures made Claudet a critical and financial success but remain interesting only for what they reveal about Victorian taste (or lack of it). Others of his portraits are worth considering for what they tell us about the nature of the photographic issues that concerned Claudet, as well as for what they tell us about his sitters.

Two family portraits, which Claudet made for different audiences, offer a good opportunity for comparison. One is a portrait of his partner Houghton with his two daughters, which he obviously did for the Houghton family, and the other is a tinted portrait of a family group, posed in his studio. In the Houghton family portrait, Claudet has constructed the photograph around a simple, triangular composition, in which the two girls are leaning on their father's shoulders. (Figure 27). The pose expresses the solidarity of the family in a clean, straightforward statement in a way that involves us with the subjects as people: the age of the girls, the book Houghton is holding, the thoughts of the children as they look inquisitively out at the viewer—all become important. Compare this portrait with one of Claudet's commercial family group portraits, which is less satisfying in all respects. This family group (Figure 28), now in the Science Museum collection, is a posed portrait of five figures who might have no relation to each other at all. Each of the figures stands stiffly, one girl on the floor, three others standing in their best clothes on a couch behind. The contrived composition does not show the relationship among the members of the family, since all are looking in different directions as if unaware of each other and seem to be concentrating on holding still for the photographer. The tinting adds a certain prettiness but does nothing to contribute to an understanding of the relationship among these people.

Claudet sometimes successfuly used painterly techniques to give a specific

---

*Claudet was the first person to use two different images of the same person in different positions to give the illusion of movement—creating, in 1852, the first known moving picture.[3]

sense of the subject's character, as in his portrait of Houghton's grandmother (Figure 29). In this case, tinting is only one aspect of the way in which the artist describes what he sees—the tinting becomes an integral part of the total conception. Another example is his fine portrait of Mrs. Andrew Pritchard, taken in September, 1847 (Figure 30). All the details, including the tinting, are visual clues about the sitter and the photographer's feelings towards her. Pastel tones, applied with a delicate hand, heighten the tranquil mood and enhance the peaceful expression on the sitter's face. Mrs. Pritchard's eyes are colored a translucent blue that corresponds with the plain blue background, giving a sense of depth to the picture, as if the distant background and the woman's thoughts are symbolically connected. Claudet has retained what appears to be a characteristic gesture, allowing the woman to play with the back of her hair. At the same time he draws attention to the subdued elegance of her costume, coloring the lace on her dress white and skillfully applying varying amounts of gold to her necklace, so that it seems finely wrought. The sitter is not beautiful according to Victorian convention, but through attention to personal detail— the hand holding a place in the book she was reading, her pensive expression— the photographer has made us aware of Mrs. Pritchard's tranquil, dignified character.

The portraits that Claudet modeled on the style of formal painted portraits appear stiff and imitative next to his perceptive character studies. His 1851 portrait of an old man (Figure 31) is identical in pose, angle of the head, even in facial expression, to a painting of the Duke of Wellington that was reproduced for popular distribution (Figure 32). Claudet failed to select any but the most superficial characteristics of the man's appearance; but he produced a likeness that would have required Andrew Robertson more than twenty-two hours of sittings with his subject for his trial portrait, ten to twelve hours for background, three on the coat, and some more time for the final painting, in a few seconds.[4]

Claudet, like Fox Talbot, had an interest in both the science and philosophy of photography. He was a vocal champion of photography as art—when he learned that the managers of the Universal Exhibition of 1862 had placed photography in the mechanical department, he wrote a furious letter to a friend:

> If photography was only a machine, such as the magic lantern, with which every one can strike pictures on a white screen with the same success, its production might indeed be exhibited in the mechanical department; but as

Figure 31. Elderly man, daguerreotype by Antoine
Claudet, c. 1851, 66 × 78 mm. (Royal Photographic
Society, London)

Figure 32. Duke of Wellington, daguerreotype from
a painting, 67 × 92 mm. (Royal Photographic Society,
London)

I find from my own experience, which is as old as photography itself, that nothing is more difficult than to produce photographs deserving to be looked at. . . I consider that there is as much art in the result as in any of the so-called fine arts.[5]

Ironically enough, Claudet's major contribution to the art of photography was considered by the critics to be his employment of a miniature painter who would doctor photographic portraits to make them palatable to Victorian tastes. Other photographers, Claudet's colleagues, were shrewder in recognizing Claudet's important contributions to both the science and art of photography.

Richard Beard, in his most successful portraits, utilizes a style devoid of color and props (painter's devices), depending on purely photographic effects to convey the essentials of his sitter's personality. Beard relied on tonal quality and detail in daguerreotype portraits as in his portrait of a young girl (Figure 33). In comparison with a portrait like Claudet's study of Mrs. Pritchard, Beard's portrait might be dismissed at first glance as a camera record of the head-and-shoulders variety. A careful look shows, however, that the subject does not seem to be posing, just glancing away from the camera, and that her features, while rather relaxed, retain a striking expressiveness. (This does not mean that a successful portrait must be one in which the subject is unaware of the camera.) The photographer's attention to detail and tone draws the viewer into a closer look at the subject. He makes us see what we might have missed—the girl's youth and freshness, her wide sensual mouth with the suggestion of a smile, her dark eyes and round dimpled chin, the young tender skin with a mole showing on her neck, and the carefully parted hair—all rendered in exquisite detail without the photographer intruding his presence on the viewer.

The British photographer Bill Brandt once defined a successful portrait photograph as an image without strong facial expression, which allows the viewer to examine the face for the character the features hold. To involve the viewer with the subject, the picture must be perfectly realized, relating form, texture, detail and feeling with accuracy. Judged by Brandt's modern criteria, Beard's nineteenth-century portrait is successful. There are no elements in the picture to divert attention from the sitter; and, in fact, we are drawn into the portrait by the essential clues that the photographer recorded. The same is true in another Beard portrait of an old lady with a lace headdress (Figure 34). The photographer tells us a great deal about the old woman in the daguerreotype by recording every line in her face and dress; once again the viewer is invited by

Figure 33. Young girl, daguerreotype by Richard Beard. (Science Museum, London)

Figure 34. Old lady with lace headdress, daguerreotype by Richard Beard. (Science Museum, London)

Figure 35. Aged man, daguerreotype by Richard Beard. (Royal Photographic Society, London)

the photographer to go beyond casual observation, into a private moment in the life of the sitter. Every ruffle in the lace headdress is clearly delineated so that the viewer can see how starched and white it is. We can also see that the woman holds her head proudly and, regardless of her age, is proud of her appearance. Beard's skill lies in his combined talent for rendering immaculate detail while preserving and recording an intimate, personal quality.

Beard's portrait of an aged man (Figure 35), in the collection of the Royal Photographic Society, is also characteristic of his best work. The portrait is uncompromisingly realistic, with no attempt made to camouflage defects or arrange the sitter in an attractive pose. The man's collar juts up awkwardly from under his whiskers, making his chin look plump and his face round, almost comical. The man's jacket hangs open, revealing his protruding stomach, and his rumpled hair has not been combed. These details, combined with the features of the sitter—his bald forehead and round face, his whiskers and plump chin—and slightly puzzled expression, contribute to the impression of a gentle and vulnerable man. Our understanding of the man's character is helped by information inherent in the basic image rather than from extras provided by the photographer.

Beard's best portraits provide a look toward future developments in portrait photography; but, for the Victorians, his photographs were merely technical exercises. This reaction should not surprise us. One can hardly expect the Victorian critics and public, confronted with a new medium, to reconsider the structure and meaning of the visual arts, especially given the conservatism of the period. Critics commented favorably only on Beard's technical aptitude:

> . . . the value of his improvements are [sic] strikingly manifested by the effects produced. For instance, the portraits taken in this way as may be expected, are much more decidedly made out, and the features have a cleanliness and strength of outline which renders them distinctly visible even by an artificial light. . . .[7]

With Claudet's photographs, critics are on more familiar ground:

> What Lawrence did with his brush, M. Claudet appears to do with his lens; he catches the best aspect of his sitter and does full justice to Nature. His female portraits have a grace and delicacy which we have never seen before in Sun portraits; his men, too, show blood; and these advantages are secured without a loss of likeness or naturalness. Such examples are a real triumph of heliographic art. What can the miniature painter—the painter of real portraits—do against the Sun?[8]

The charm and quaintness of the portraits which the Victorians themselves preferred and the interest these portraits have as an historical record should not blind the viewer to Beard's quite different contribution. His early experiments with the unmanipulated image have an important place in the artistic development of the photographic medium.

The Victorians accepted photography because they found it useful, and then, in the fashion typical of the period, disguised its utilitarianism by attributing artistic value to it. William Edward Kilburn, a daguerreotypist in London who began his professional career in 1848, mastered this art of disguise. His photographs closely resembled miniature paintings; in fact, his particular skill was using the photographic image as a guideline to paint over so that the photographic qualities were completely obliterated. Kilburn's portraits were sentimental and pretty, but they had the advantage over minature paintings of being true to "nature," rapidly produced, and less expensive. Immediately popular with the portrait-happy public, Kilburn also became a favorite of the critics:

> We had admirable studies by Mr. Kilburn in Daguerreotype, totally unlike those usually seen in London or the Palais Royal. The artist has succeeded in using color with all the delicacy and gradation essential to the representation of flesh . . .[9]

No mention was made, of course, of Mr. Kilburn's skill as a photographer or as a portraitist. A month later the same reviewer was to tell us: "Mr. Kilburn has called in the assistance of a practised miniature painter who understands the means which he employs both chemically and artistically."[10] (We can see that Kilburn has been praised in the first instance for a skill he himself did not have.) He did have a shrewd business sense, and a practical mind—the camera became, in his hands, a tool for mass-producing imitation miniature paintings.

Kilburn developed a particular style for children, another for ladies, and a

Figure 36. A child, daguerreotype by William Kilburn. (Science Museum, London)

third for gentlemen, styles which he duplicated for all his clients. His photograph of a child, from the Science Museum (Figure 36), typifies these imitation miniatures: This child, her hair tinted golden blond, is portrayed in a lace-edged dress which shows her rosy (tinted) young shoulders. The background of sky and clouds is painted striking blue and white—it appears that the child is sitting outside. Even the elaborate frame was fashioned in the oval shape of most miniature paintings. In Kilburn's portrait of a lady (Figure 37), we have an appropriate title, because all of Kilburn's female sitters were made to look as if they embodied the ideal of Victorian womanhood. This lady was posed in an artificial set, complete with a pillar, a brocade chair, and a painted sky backdrop. These props, which imply wealth, were copied from the artifacts usually found in miniature paintings. In the days when only the wealthiest could afford to commission portraits, these props were probably indicative of the sitter's lifestyle, but in Kilburn's studio they served as a fashionable exaggeration. The prettiness of this portrait, the tinted blue sky matched with the lady's blue dress, the gilt paint on the lady's jewelry and on the brocade chair, seem to have been adequate compensation for the lack of character in the sitter's face, at least in the eyes of the Victorian client.

It is difficult to believe that Kilburn's portrait of a gentleman (Figure 38) is not a miniature painting, because the camera was used exclusively to record an outline on which to paint. The subject was posed with exaggerated formality, head erect and arm resting on a chair with a book clasped in his hand. Elaborate coloring has completely obliterated the photographic image—the man's eyes are blue, his cheeks pink, the brocade chair is red, the sky lavender, and the gold clasp at his waistcoat is tinted. Unlike Claudet's use of tinting, this coloration lacks subtlety and provides the viewer with no distinguishable personal information about the sitter.

Claudet's and Kilburn's tinted portraits met with precisely the same response from critics and the public, although the similarities in their work are superficial. We even find Richard Beard being praised in similar terms once he began to use color. In 1846 a reviewer writes of Beard's portraits:

> We would especially notice the admirable effect of the flesh tints which appear as if actually embodied in the miniature, and not as we generally see them spread on the surface. Among the specimens submitted to our inspection we discerned the freshness of beauty and life in some, the unequivocal characteristics of thought and intellect in others.[11]

These portraits, although skillfully tinted, do not have the direct impact of

Figure 37. A lady, daguerreotype by William Kilburn. (Science Museum, London)

Figure 38. A gentleman, daguerreotype by William Kilburn. (Science Museum, London)

Beard's detailed and subtle, unmanipulated daguerreotypes. At the time, however, they were certainly considered the more "artistic."

The Victorian critic can best teach us ways *not* to look at photographs. The early photographers were already beginning to show an awareness of characteristics that were inherent to the photographic medium and to make choices based on that awareness: Beard discarded applied color for the simpler, more graphic tones of his later and best pictures. Claudet used the calotype and found it unsatisfactory—he vacillated between commerce and art, tinted and straight images. Both men were learning what they could and could not do with the camera. Their critics remained stolidly unaware that the photographer, not his instruments, made the picture. Like Claudet's reviewer, who compared the creator of "real" pictures with the Sun, John Ruskin concluded, in *The Stones of Venice* in 1851, that photography could not be art because the process was purely mechanical:

> All art is good and true only so far as it is distinctively the work of manhood in its entire and highest sense; that is to say, not the work of limbs and fingers, but of the soul, aided, according to her necessities, by the inferior powers...a photograph is not a work of art, though it requires certain delicate manipulations of paper and acid and subtle calculations of time... so neither would a drawing like a photograph, made directly from nature be a work of art...[12]

His initial misconception, that the camera makes the photograph (which leaves the stylistic differences between Beard and Claudet unexplained), was a short step away from the graver error—that "art" could be applied to the photograph in brushstrokes, and the finer the photograph, the more it resembled a painting in style and content.

Even today, so little has been done in the field of photographic criticism that a review of a major photography exhibition is rarely written without a comparison between modern photography and some aspect of painting. (In certain cases, for example, a discussion of early twentieth-century photography and impressionism—a comparison is justified historically by the symbiotic relationship that existed between the two media.) Mostly however, the value of a photograph is still gauged by the degree to which it resembles something other than a photograph. Perhaps when we look back on this time as part of photography's early history, modern critics will seem as misguided in their approach as their forerunners at *The Art Union*. In the meantime, with our knowledge of the mistakes of the first critics of photography, it should be possible to avoid some of their pitfalls and come to historical photographs with a fresh, unprejudiced eye.

Minor White, in *Aperture,* suggested a method of understanding single photographs, which he called "reading." White, who regarded each photograph as a complex structure of meanings, believed that photographic analysis could best be achieved by determined contemplation, so that the viewer is forced to come to terms with only the information given by the photograph itself.[11] He stipulated certain criteria: that the image transcend its original purpose and go beyond instinctive subject, emotional manner, and intellectual information. White's theory applies only to single photographs, and only to photographs like his own, which are designed to trigger the viewer's imagination to transcend literal reality. In no way did White intend for his method to apply to historical photographs. With his method, the photograph must be deeply felt and experienced by the viewer for its significance to outweigh value judgment. In the case of historical photographs, the concern is not so much with the spiritual significance of the photograph as with the relation of past work to present developments in the medium. However, the concept of "reading" can facilitate an examination of photographs that have historical as well as visual importance. The importance of reading is that the viewer is forced to go to the image itself for information—with the aim of understanding rather than evaluating. In this way he can free himself from the misconceptions that result from acceptance of dated and visually unsophisticated critical opinions.

In the process of reading historical photographs, the viewer might concentrate on the four categories considered below. These categories are not designed to interfere with the spontaneous process of looking at photographs and are expected to enhance rather than obliterate the viewer's own immediate and private response. The categories are listed separately for the purpose of discussion and clarification: First, *what is the subject of the photograph?* To define the subject necessitates temporarily ignoring the *way* in which the photographer describes what he sees, and concentrating on *what* he sees. Especially in the case of old photographs, which initially charm the viewer with the flavor of the era, the strange costumes, hairstyles, formal poses, and outdated technical processes all tend to obfuscate the basic subject. The viewer should look for every clue about the subject—it is not enough to identify the sitter as a Victorian lady, or an old lady, or an old lady in a black dress. How does this particular old lady hold her hands? Is her pose natural to her, are there noticeably characteristic gestures, or has the pose been contrived by the photographer? What can be learned from her expression, her eyes, the angle of her body? What makes this old lady different from every other lady we have seen portrayed?

The next step is *assessing the feeling* of the photograph—the *bias* of the photographer to his subject. Had he some special interest in an aspect of the person or a special relationship with the sitter? The photograph will reveal some personal coloring; it may be indicated simply by the camera angle chosen, or by softness or harshness of lighting. The portrait represents one individual seen uniquely by another individual.

Closely related is the photographer's *attitude toward the viewer*. The image is designed to trigger certain responses in the person looking at the picture. Our actual response is of course often determined by other criteria than those intended by the photographer. For instance, a landscape might remind us of a childhood haunt, or a facial expression might stimulate us to remember an old friend. These responses, although important to our individual experience in looking at pictures, are not valid in terms of understanding what the artist wishes us to see. The viewer must look for the specific, unique treatment of the subject, belonging only to that particular image. The viewer should consider both what the photographer included and what he edited from the image. For instance, did the photographer emphasize the lines and wrinkles on an old woman's face, or did he emphasize the softly lighted air around her?

The final step is to make an assumption about the *meaning* of the photograph. Often subjects have meaning attached to them by traditional association—for example, we might associate an old woman with wisdom and experience. Based on clues drawn from the three categories of *subject, feeling,* and *attitude,* the viewer should be able to make a judgment concerning *the experience the photograph was made to illustrate.* A specific rather than a traditional meaning should be apparent—a sense of the significance of the particular moment captured by the photographer.

With such an approach, the possible interpretations open to the viewer are extensive, and it is by no means easy to know whether the insight gained is valid in terms of the photographer's feeling and intention. Regardless of the degree of accuracy, however, the effort to read photographs using the information provided by the images themselves (with the aim of understanding rather than evaluation) is useful. Besides helping the viewer break away from the biases of a dated critical approach, reading images tends to keep the viewer from relying solely on a personal intuitive reaction as a guide to appreciating the photographs.

Notes

1. Charles Baudelaire, quoted in Alex Strasser, *Immortal Portraits,* London, 1848, p. 46.

2. London Post Office Directory, Guildhall Library, London.

3. Arthur Gill, *Antoine François Jean Claudet,* Royal Photographic Society pamphlet, p. 6.

4. Raymond Lister, *The British Miniature,* Pitman and Sons, London, 1951.

5. *British Journal of Photography,* "Claudet—A Memoir," Sept. 11, 1868, pp. 437–39.

6. In a personal interview with the author, London, March 1974.

7. *The Art-Union,* April 15, 1841, p. 65.

8. *Athenaeum,* August 30, 1846.

9. *Athenaeum,* March 20, 1847.

10. *Athenaeum,* April 17, 1847.

11. *The Art-Union,* May 1, 1846, p. 139.

12. R. N. Watson, "Art, Photography and John Ruskin," *British Journal of Photography,* March 10, 1944.

13. John Ward, *The Criticism of Photography As Art: The Photographs of Jerry Uelsmann,* University of Florida Humanities Monograph, No. 32, p. 11.

4
The Photographer and Society

For the past century or more we have seen our history through photographs. It is difficult to imagine a time when we could read about but not see presidents, queens and kings, actors and actresses, socialites, authors, musicians, criminals or tycoons—and even stranger to remember that until this century, most people did not know what their ancestors looked like. Before photography, one of the many distinctions between the British upper class and the rest of society was that they alone possessed a visual link with the past—those painted ancestral portraits which established beyond doubt that certain families were a significant part of the flow of history. Daguerre's announcement changed all that—photography was the great leveller—because to the undiscriminating eye of the camera lens, everyone looked relatively alike. Inevitably, however, the art of portrait photography became stratified along nineteenth-century class lines: Big business in photography centered around the upwardly mobile middle class who recognized, with an eye to history, that photography might be another passport into the social arena. Soon even the working class acquired a breed of photographer, the street-corner operator who would "take yer 'ead for sixpence" while other photographers specialized in creating fantastical images for the rich and famous. The result is that the photographs left us from the Victorian past document the social structure as much as they portray the individuals who were part of it.

Royal recognition of any invention assured its acceptance by the middle class public, and Victoria and Albert set the example by continually sitting for photographers and by sending photographs as gifts to all their friends and relations. From the earliest days of photography, the Royal Family took a strong interest in its progress—in fact the story is told that the day Victoria proposed to Albert, to allay her nervousness, she talked to him first about Daguerre's newly published invention. Prince Albert posed for a daguerreo-typist whose identity is unknown as early as March 6, 1842, in Brighton when he and the Queen were staying at the Royal Pavillion, according to the Queen's diary.[1] By 1847 the Royal family had attempted a daguerreotype group portrait, with results that far from satisfied the Queen:

> We both sat in the greenhouse [in Buckingham Palace] to Mr. Killburn [sic] for Daguerotypes [sic] which are not much improved to what they originally were. Mine was really very successful. Those of the children were unfortunately entire failures.[2]

(The children most likely had difficulty sitting still for the long exposure time.) Five years later Kilburn was recalled to photograph the Royal Family at Windsor, and this time Victoria wrote: "The day was splendid for it. Mine was unfortunately horrid but the children's were pretty."[3] In acknowledgment of his achievements as a photographer, Victoria appointed Kilburn the first of many Photographists To Her Majesty And His Royal Highness, giving official recognition to photography and significant status to photographers.

Victoria and Albert initiated the use of photography to commemorate all important public and private occasions, usually in the form of a portrait photograph—the Prince of Wales on his confirmation day, Victoria and Albert at every anniversary and birthday celebration, the family mourning the death of Albert. Aside from the historical interest these photographs hold, they represent the first time that the public was permitted to see their leaders in private moments of pleasure and sorrow. Royal portraits were taken both by amateurs, such as Prince Albert's librarian, Dr. E. Becker, and one of his equerries, Captain Dudley (later Lord) de Ros, and by professionals—Antoine, Claudet, Bambridge, Caldesi, W. and D. Downey, Hills and Saunders, J. J. E. Mayall, and T. R. Williams. The photographer most often at family events was George Washington Wilson of Aberdeen, who was able to photograph the Royal Family at play, at the Queen's favorite retreat, Balmoral Castle in Scotland. Wilson's first commission, to photograph the castle in 1854, was so well received by Victoria that she sent Wilson to take an historic group

Figure 39. Queen Victoria and Prince Albert, by Roger Fenton, 1854. (Victoria and Albert Museum, London)

Figure 40. Queen Victoria by Roger Fenton, salted paper, c. 1854. (Royal Photographic Society, London)

Figure 41. Royal family group at Balmoral, by George Washington Wilson, September 29, 1855, with (left to right) Prince Frederick William of Prussia, Prince Alfred, Princess Helena, Price of Wales, Princess Alice, Queen Victoria, Princess Royal, Princess Louise, Prince Albert.

This photograph was taken on the day the Princess Royal became engaged to Prince Frederick William of Prussia. Reproduced by Gracious Permission of Her Majesty Queen Elizabeth II. (Royal Library, Windsor Castle) portrait on the day Prince Frederick William of Prussia proposed to the Princess Royal. Victoria appointed Wilson the Photographer Royal for Scotland in 1860, after which he recorded the family at some of their most intimate moments. One of Wilson's most touching portraits shows Queen Victoria with Princess Louis of Hess (Princess Alice) and Princess Helena, grouped in front of a painting of the Prince Consort, mourning his death in solitude but for the camera and the photographer. Of course, these mourning portraits immediately became the fashion in England.

The royal nod of approval was the final spur to a public already, as described by one observer, "portrait-mad," and within a few years, the photography business had a booming market. Photographers cleverly capitalized on the fragility of the daguerreotype, which was one of its major drawbacks, by devising elaborate packaging—cases and mounts sent the cost of the original image spiralling with prices starting at £1.05.[4] Early daguerreotypes were sold in Morocco cases, consisting of a gilt mat, a covering glass, and a pinchback frame; but as the demand for portraits grew, British photographers began to make use of the American Union case, which could be made to look more elaborate and therefore cost more. Union cases, used for portraits until the turn of the century, consisted of a mixture of shellac and papier-maché or sawdust, which was heated and pressed into a mold, usually based on the design of a popular painting. When the mixture was cool, the fine detail of the dye was retained into a hardened compound.[5] Items of jewelry, including lockets, pendants, rings, tie-pins, even cuff-links, were also decorated with daguerreotype portraits. Memorial brooches, used for the remembrance of a dead relative, contained daguerreotypes of the person, photographed either dead or alive.

The only problem facing the photographer was satisfying the overwhelming public demand. The daguerreotype yielded only one copy, and the calotype, which yielded limitless copies, could not compete with the fine detail of the daguerreotype image. In 1851, Frederick Scott Archer, a sculptor working in Tavistock Street, published details of a new process, which in a few years would make both the daguerreotype and the calotype extinct. Archer had tried numerous methods of using collodion to improve the surface of the paper, but the first collodion picture taken on glass resulted from a careless error. Unable to remove a collodion film from the glass plate he was working on, Archer made the best of a bad job by sensitizing and exposing the film while it was still attached to the plate. The results of this experiment led him to perfect the process which he published in *The Chemist*, in 1851.

Figure 42. Frederick Scott Archer, a glass collodion portrait, by A. H. Cade. (Science Museum, London)

The collodion process was surprisingly simple: collodion was made by dissolving gun-cotton in ether containing a little alcohol. This was oxidized and poured onto a glass plate, which was then dropped into a solution of silver nitrate to become sensitized. After a few minutes, the wet plate was placed in the dark slide of a camera and exposed, and once removed, was developed and fixed for permanence.[6]

Almost immediately, the wet collodion process replaced all other photographic processes—not only did it yield a negative of exceptionally high quality, but it was more sensitive to light, making portraiture quicker and easier. Tens of thousands practiced collodion portraiture, in every town and village, in England and abroad. Fortunes could be made overnight, and the census of 1861 reveals that the number of professional photographers in England had grown from 51 to 2,534 in ten years.[7] Ironically, Archer left his own family destitute because he refused to secure the collodion process by patent, believing that his experiment was valuable to all the world. Archer was one of the few photographers of the period who did not realize his fortune by it.

Novelty portraits became big business. In 1854, the Parisian photographer Disderi introduced the visiting card photograph, an albumen silver print (2¼″ × 3½″) pasted on to a card (2½″ × 4″). The craze for *cartes-de-visites* (Figures 43–46) spread to England, where it was estimated several hundred million of them were sold in the 1860's alone. People amassed portraits, not only of friends and relatives, but of royalty, celebrities, newsmakers, and scandalmakers, and filed them in elaborately decorated albums. For many Victorians, these portraits represented glamour and excitement, a ticket into an unknown world, serving a purpose similar to the modern movie magazine. Owning the image of a famous actor or actress enabled the collector to share in another person's life, in a small but intimate way. As may be imagined, with the first voyeuristic thrill of seeing Mayall's At Home portraits of celebrities, or Camille da Silvy's carte-de-visite portraits of the Beauties of England, the general public demanded that their photographs indicate a similar standard of living. Portrait studios acquired elaborate backdrops and theatrical props, painted Gothic arches and velvet drapery, imitation antiques, entire stage sets of drawing rooms and sumptuous gardens. Before long, a tailor's wife from Liverpool could be photographed in front of silk curtains and (imitation) stone pillars, just like the Queen herself (Figure 47).

Celebrity portraits were introduced to England by an American, John Edwin Mayall, who, aware of the popularity for royal portraits in France,

Figures 43–46. (Science Museum, London)

Figure 47. Portrait of a woman dressed as the Queen. (Science Museum, London)

Figure 50. Princess Alice as "Spring." Reproduced by Gracious Permission of Her Majesty Queen Elizabeth II. (Royal Library, Windsor Castle)

Figure 51. Prince Alfred as "Autumn." Reproduced by Gracious Permission of Her Majesty Queen Elizabeth II. (Royal Library, Windsor Castle)

Figure 52. Royal family in mourning for Prince Albert, by Bambridge, March 28, 1862 at Windsor Castle, with Queen Victoria, Crown Princess of Prussia, Princess Alice, and Prince Alfred. Reproduced by Gracious Permission of Her Majesty Queen Elizabeth II. (Royal Library, Windsor Castle)

Family, which record them at home at their leisure. Fenton, a painter and solicitor who became famous for his photographs of the Crimean War, was responsible for the founding of the first Photographic Society in England. Fenton was probably introduced to Victoria and Albert by Prince Albert's librarian, Dr. Becker, who was also a founder member of the Society. Both men were aware that royal approval would legitimize their society, and in 1853, Fenton persuaded the Queen and Prince Consort to become patrons. After that, Fenton brought his camera to Buckingham Palace on many private family occasions—the photographs he made leave us with a curious record of the tastes and pleasures of Victorian royalty. Fenton photographed the children in a series of *tableaux vivants* taken during the fourteenth anniversary celebration for Victoria and Albert, on February 10, 1854. Dressed in costume, the children recited extracts from James Thompson's poem "The Seasons." Afterwards Fenton grouped them in suitable poses: laconically standing in front of skindraped tables on a leaf-strewn floor, arranged in groups with leopard skin and leaves over their clothes and wreaths around their heads. These photographs were taken for the pleasure of the family and not intended for publication. When, years after Fenton's death, one of the portraits was published by a relation of the Royal Family, Queen Victoria was furious and insisted the negative be destroyed.

The wet collodion process made it possible to produce photographs in quantity, and many photographers did so, acting as publishers. In 1859, the photographers Maull and Polyblank finally published a completed version of the photographic portrait gallery attempted by Herbert Fry.[1] The gallery, called *Photographic Portraits of Living Celebrities*, followed Fry's format of portrait and written biography and included David Livingstone (Figure 53), the Archbishop of Canterbury, Samuel Wilberforce (Figure 54), and other statesmen, artists, actors, and aristocrats. The photographers did not concern themselves with character interpretation beyond the most obvious touches: the naturalist Richard Owen (Figure 55) holds a fossil skull of a prehistoric animal; composer William Sterndale Bennet, baton in hand, leans on a music stand. Rarely does the vitality of the sitter penetrate the wooden pose and conventional setting.

The distinction should be drawn between those photographers who saw portrait photography as a business venture and those who took advantage of the enthusiasm and naiveté of the public. These "street-corner" photographers preyed on clients who could not afford the fancier studios of Mayall or Kilburn and who were unaware that skill and craftsmanship were needed to operate the

Photographer. " Now, Sir ! Ave yer Cart de Visit done ? "

From *Punch in Cameraland,* W. & J. Mackay & Co. Ltd, Chatham, 1948
Courtesy *Punch Magazine.*

camera. Henry Mayhew, in his famous study written in 1851, *London Labour and the London Poor,* characterizes just such a charlatan:

> I never knew anything about taking portraits then, though they showed me when I bought the apparatus (but that was as good as nothing, for it takes months to learn). But I had the cards ready printed before I bought the apparatus. The very next day I had the camera, I had a customer before I had even tried it, so I tried it on him, and I gave him a black picture (for I didn't know how to make the portrait and it was all black when I took the glass out), and told him that it would become brighten as it dried, and he went away quite delighted.[11]

Street-corner photography was common in most towns in Britain, and in most cases, the portraits produced amounted to a mere outline of the face of the sitter, the images fading within an hour after shooting. Some photographers

Photographic Portraits

OF

LIVING CELEBRITIES;

Executed by

MAULL AND POLYBLANK;

With Biographical Notices

BY E. WALFORD, M.A.,

LATE SCHOLAR OF BALLIOL COLLEGE, OXFORD, AND FELLOW OF THE GENEALOGICAL AND HISTORICAL SOCIETY OF GREAT BRITAIN.

VOL. I.

London:

MAULL & POLYBLANK, 55, GRACECHURCH STREET, & 187A, PICCADILLY.

W. KENT & CO., 86, FLEET STREET.

1859.

Advertisement for Maull and Polyblank Photographic Portraits of Living Celebrities

Maull and Polyblank, Photographic Portraits of Living Celebrities

(Vol. I, 1859. Published as a book with 40 portrait
photographs, by W. Kent and Co., London)

Figure 53. Reverend Dr. David Livingstone, 7¾″ × 5¾″. (Museum of Modern Art, N.Y.)

Figure 54. Samuel Wilberforce, Lord Bishop of Oxford, 7¾″ × 5¾″. (Museum of Modern Art, N.Y.)

Figure 55. Professor Richard Owen, 7¾″ × 5¾″. (Museum of Modern Art, N.Y.)

95

Figure 56. Daniel Maclise Esq., 7¾″ × 5¾″. (Museum of Modern Art, N.Y.)

gave their clients portraits of other sitters, telling them the face would grow to look more like their own as time passed; others hired "doormen" who amounted to little more than thugs, for the purpose of luring or forcing clients into their studios.

The situation grew so bad that, by the middle 1850s, portrait photography was associated with these nuisances and charlatans, and serious photographers were implored, in the words of the photographer Adam-Solomon, to "make photography fit for society."[12] The very enthusiasm which nurtured the growth of photography by encouraging experimentation and invention nearly caused its ruin, so horrified was the public by these vulgar charlatans calling themselves photographers. An editorial from the *Daily Telegraph* of 1861 illustrates this public concern:

PHOTOGRAPHIC DENS AND DOORSMEN: Our censure is directed against the low dens of cheap photography, with which even the most respectable of our thoroughfares are becoming infested. There is a duplicate system of ruffianism in these disgraceful places. There is the 'professor' or 'manipulator' or 'focusser' or whatever he may call himself who keeps in the doghole he terms a 'studio,' who executes vile libels on humanity which he misnames portraits.[13]

The article goes on to tell of bullied women and terrified children, forced to buy expensive frames for their fading portraits, and pleads for an act of Parliament to remove "this atrocious nuisance." The problem could have been remedied, not by an act of Parliament, but by informing the public about the complexities of the photographic process—commentators still emphasized the speed with which photography could make imitation miniatures, rather than the knowledge, skill, creative decision, and taste needed to produce a satisfactory picture. As long as the public wanted cheap, fast portraits, they were to suffer at the hands of cheap, tasteless exploiters.

Many of the cases involving these portrait dens are shocking and inexcusable. Mrs. Catherine Anthony, the wife of a pay sergeant of the Fusilier Guards, was reported to have gone into the photographic shop of William Pimms in Oxford Street to have her portrait taken for a brooch. When she objected to the finished product and refused to purchase it, she was struck on the head by Mr. Pimms until she was unconscious. He then tore up the portrait, pushed her downstairs, and ordered the "doorman" to attack her as well. This particular case was brought to court and the photographer fined £5.[14] Appar-

Figure 65. Duchess of Cambridge with her daughter Princess Mary of Cambridge (later the Duchess of Teck), October 5, 1860.

three-quarter view which shows, not only Miss Warren's back, but a landscape scene that she appears to be looking toward. The elements of this portrait balance perfectly, the latticed window at the left acting as a counterweight to a second portrait of Miss Warren framed in the mirror. Both serve to emphasize the central full-figure portrait of the sitter. The portrait forces us to shift our attention from the immediate subject to the scene behind, which in turn triggers the imagination as to what is actually in front of the sitter, out of the boundaries of the mirror's reflection.

One of Silvy's specialties seemed to be producing portraits to his client's specification. In the case of Lady Mary Craven, Silvy was obviously requested to create a portrait of a lady overcome with grief, and he did so with his usual finesse (Figure 61). On the right side of the portrait, the sitter stands bathed in shadow. Her face, seen in profile, looks tragic. One hand touches her throat, as if to force back her sobs, while the other hangs at her side limply holding a single lily. Her face, her hand and the flower appear pale in contrast to the shadow and her dark mourning costume. The woman's face, reflected in a mirror, reveals the grief she tries to hide by turning her head away—but the mirror softens tone and detail so that her pathetic expression is somehow extremely flattering.

A series of portraits of a group of ladies shows them dressed to represent various virtues: Truth, Prudence, Faith, and so on. This sort of performance was typical of the fashion of the period for theatrical sketches of moral value, and Silvy contributed splendidly to the theme, with lovely stage sets and lighting. *Faith* is a masterpiece of craftsmanship, picturing a windblown figure carrying a cross and posed beneath a starry sky (Figure 63).

We cannot help but wonder what Silvy thought of his English clients, with their peculiar Victorian preference for moralizing and storytelling. Some of his portraits seem to indicate a subtle tongue-in-cheek attitude, as in the portrait of Thomas Price, Esq. (Figure 64). The man has a fiercely determined expression, sitting leg crossed, shoulders square and his face rigid, staring stonily to the right of the picture. Directly beside him, Silvy had placed a stone bust of a man's head, with an expression that was as stony, determined, and stubborn as Mr. Price's. The resemblance might be dismissed as coincidental, did we not know the care with which Silvy placed every prop and arranged every picture.

The same humor, whether intended or not, is present in the portrait of Her Royal Highness the Duchess of Cambridge with Her Royal Highness Princess Mary of Cambridge, which is probably unsurpassed as a character study of

Victorian British royalty (Figure 65). Silvy posed the pair before a beautifully elaborate painted set of a palatial staircase, which cuts from the left of the picture back to the right, leading the eye to the two central figures in the foreground. The figures are difficult to miss as they are grouped together, in full outdoor dress complete with hats and shawls, forming a massive solid bulk. The walls are illustrated with classical scenes, balanced by another artificial backdrop of a painted archway and an alcove with painted books. Silvy recreated an atmosphere sufficiently opulent to suit a duchess and a princess, but he seems not to have sought a modification of their expressions—severe, tightlipped, narrow eyed—which are noticeably puritanical compared with the lavish, sumptuous environment. Silvy added the same sort of props in this portrait as appeared in Price's portrait. On the table beside the two figures, Silvy placed a charming statue on a pillar, which appears to be two naked cherubim with their arms around each other. Silvy may have intended to balance the composition by including the statue, but one cannot help but laugh at the contrast between the two couples.

Other studios of the period could not compare to Silvy's luxurious mansion and personal service. Elliott and Fry's studio in Baker Street was described by one observer in 1865:

> There were three studios, the smallest for vignettes. The light is easterly, and the main feature is an elongated canopy stretched over the cameras, 12 feet long, so that the photographer looked at the sitter through a tunnel.[18]

Fry's technique was as unpretentious as his studio. The rule of the establishment was to keep the sitter in the glass-house for no longer than ten minutes, so that after a brief period of time while Fry tried to relax the sitter, he shot one or two portraits and dismissed his client. Fry relied on skill rather than luck, to the surprise of one sitter who protested, "You cannot have secured a good portrait for I was only taken twice during the few minutes I was in the glass room. Usually they take ten or fifteen of me before they get it right."[19]

The studios of W. and D. Downey, located near Buckingham Palace, were slightly less spartan. The public could walk directly into the glass-house from the street, at which point they found themselves facing one blank wall, the other three walls and the ceiling being made out of ground glass. The room was usually bathed in soft illumination, but in winter or dull weather, the roof could be removed to enhance the light. The studio was fitted to represent a modest drawing room—the wall was light lavender with a panelling of ground glass around the skirting. Curtains were added or removed to the client's taste, and movable screens were used for casting shadows. Obviously, Messrs. Downey could not compete with the lavishness of Silvy's establishment, but they too produced a collection of celebrity photographs which were avidly consumed by the buying public.

Perhaps the true secret of Silvy's success was that he was a master of fantasy, in an age when reality was often harsh and unpalatable. The middle class patrons of Downey's studios were content with images that recorded their facial features, for indeed this was a great stride forward for people who had previously only known their faces from the family mirror. But Victorian society revolved around a social order—children looked up to their parents, women to their husbands, men to their Queen, and to God. Ordinary people expected the camera to record their faces as ordinary, but how unpleasant it would have been to discover that one's heroes and heroines were ordinary too. Silvy portrayed the ruling class, partly in answer to his client's requirements, but mostly for the viewing public, in a way that was pure fantasy. In so doing, he showed the Victorian public that the camera was more than nature's mirror in the hands of a skilled and talented craftsman.

*   *   *

From his shoulder Hiawatha
Took the camera of rosewood;
Made of sliding, folding rosewood;
Neatly put it all together
It its case it lay compactly
Folded into nearly nothing;
But he opened out the hinges,
Pushed and pulled the joints and hinges,
Till it looked all squares and oblongs,
Like a complicated figure
In the Second Book of Euclid.
This he perched upon a tripod—
Crouched beneath its dusky cover—
Stretched his hand, enforcing silence—
Said, "Be motionless, I beg you".

—from *Hiawatha's Photographing,* 1857
by Lewis Carroll

Notes

1. Helmut Gernsheim, *Victoria R: a biography.* New York, Putnam, 1959, p. 257.

2. *Ibid,* p. 258.

3. *Ibid.*

4. Kodak Museum, Harrow and Wealdstone, Middlesex. G. B.

5. *Ibid.*

6. Science Museum Photography Collection Catalogue, London, 1969, p. 64-65.

7. *Ibid.,* p. 65.

8. Helmut Gernsheim, *Victoria R: a biography,* New York, Putnam, 1959, p. 261.

9. Gail Buckland and Cecil Beaton, *The Magic Image,* Little Brown & Company, Boston, 1975, p. 49.

10. Photographic Portraits of Living Celebrities, executed by Maull & Polyblank with Biographical Notices by E. Walford MA, Vol. 1, 1859, Museum of Modern Art, New York.

11. Henry Mayhew, *Mayhew's Characters,* William Kimber & Co., London, 1951, p. 269 ff. (A group of essays selected from *London Labour, London Poor,* edited by Peter Quennel). The first documentary photographs, which are no longer in existence, were daguerreotypes by Richard Beard of street types to illustrate Mayhew's *London Labour and the London Poor,* in which they were copied as woodcuts.

12. Alex Strasser, *Immortal Portraits,* London, 1848, p. 52.

13. *Photographic News,* August 16, 1861, p. 389.

14. *Ibid.,* p. 384.

15. The distinctive mark of the laboring man was that he worked with his hands. No matter how skilled he was or how high his earnings, his social status was determined by the kind of job he performed. Figures from the period estimate the laboring classes totalled over 4 million plus wives and children, and 1 million domestic servants. The middle classes of the 1840s and 1850s thought of themselves as an island, surrounded by a sea of poverty.

16. According to Harrison, upper class British were wealthy owners of land: (1) aristocracy—estate owners (dukes, marquises, earls, viscounts, barons); heads of families forming the Peerage and sitting in House of Lords; (2) country gentry—village squires, knights, baronets; (3) gentlemen—gentle birth, ownership of landed estate, income sufficient to permit enjoyment of leisure.

17. Helmut and Alison Gernsheim, *The History of Photography,* Thames & Hudson, London, 1965, p. 297.

18. H. Baden Pritchard, *Studios of Europe,* London 1901, p. 44.

19. Quoted in *ibid.*

5
The Victorian Amateur

The English character is as varied as its landscape—which may explain why a society blanketed by strait-laced prudery and convention should produce such talented eccentrics as Julia Margaret Cameron and Lewis Carroll. If we define amateur to mean the opposite of professional, one who works for love rather than money, then Cameron and Carroll would qualify; and yet strictly speaking, neither one was working for the love of the craft. These two seemed to be motivated by an obsessive interest in their sitters, but this emphasis on subject rather than process was not necessarily characteristic of the amateur. In general, the Victorian amateur might be described as having a life aside from photography: Charles L. Dodgson (Lewis Carroll) was a mathematics lecturer at Oxford, and Cameron did not begin to photograph until she was well into middle age and had raised a family. Some photographers were also painters and at least one—Hugh Welch Diamond—was a doctor, in charge of a hospital for mental patients. In almost every case, the zeal they shared made photography figure in their lives as much more than a pastime.

An astonishing feature of Julia Margaret Cameron's photographs is that they cannot be imitated. Among the mass of genre photographs and soft-focus portraits of people costumed for Victorian theatricals, Cameron's photographs remain unique in the impact of their heightened feeling. Sir Henry Taylor wrote of Cameron: "She lives upon superlatives as on her daily bread. . ."[1] It is the quality of intensification—heightening the beauty of every person she photographed to the greatest degree possible—that makes Cameron's work vital.

She was born Julia Margaret Pattle, in 1815, to a well-to-do English family living in Calcutta. In 1838 she married Charles Hay Cameron. Ten years later the Camerons were established in Freshwater, on the Isle of Wight, where Julia Cameron kept open house for many of the great writers and artists of the day. She probably would have remained content, participating in the arts as patron rather than artist, had not her son and daughter-in-law given her a camera. Immediately Cameron, then fifty years old, declared that her true purpose in life was to create beauty. She turned her coal-house into a darkroom, her fowl-house into a glass-house studio, and proceeded to photograph everyone she could lay hands on.

Her first portrait, *Annie*, (Figure 66) was a photograph of a young girl called Annie Philpot. Cameron recorded the momentous occasion in her diary in January 1864: "I was in a transport of delight . . . I ran all over the house to search for gifts for the child. I felt as if she had entirely made the picture. . ."[2] In the months that followed, Cameron produced vast quantities of portraits. Mary Hillier, her parlormaid, was a constant model, either alone in a close-up or surrounded by children in anecdotal photographs entitled *Contemplation, Madonna Pensosa* (Figure 67), and others of similar sentiment. These genre photographs were more an outlet for Cameron's emotional energy than portraits, and yet they contain much of the passion and sentiment of her most moving portrait studies. That she was seeking a release for her creative feelings in photography is evident and in true Victorian spirit she poured these feelings into classical scenes or moral tales. A letter written by Cameron's niece, Lady Troubridge, gives an idea of the kind of experience a sitting for Cameron must have been:

> To me, I frankly own, Aunt Julia appeared as a terrifying elderly woman, short and squat, with none of the Pattle grace and beauty about her. Dressed in dark clothing, stained with chemicals from her photography (and smelling of them too), with a plump eager face and piercing eyes, and a voice husky and a little harsh, yet in some way compelling and even charming. We were at once pressed into service of the camera. Our roles were no less than those of two Angels of the Nativity, and to sustain them we were scantily clad and each had a pair of heavy wings fastened to her narrow shoulders, while Aunt Julia, with ungentle hand, touzled our hair

Figure 66. Annie Philpot ("My first success"), January, 1864, 5½″ × 7½″. (Royal Photographic Society, London)

Figure 67. "Madonna Pensosa." (Metropolitan Museum of Art, Harris Brisbane Dick Fund, N.Y.)

Figure 68. Sir John Herschel (1792–1871), 1867 at Collingwood, his own residence, 10½″ × 13½″. (Metropolitan Museum of Art, N.Y.)

Figure 69. Charles Darwin (1809–1882), c. 1868, 9″ × 11″. (Metropolitan Museum of Art, N.Y., David Hunter McAlpin Fund.)

Figure 70. Thomas Carlyle (1795–1881), at Little Holland House, 1867, 9¼″ × 11¾″, (Metropolitan Museum of Art, N.Y., Gift of the Estate of Alfred Stieglitz Collection.)

Figure 71. Henry Wadsworth Longfellow (1807–1882), 1868, 10 × 13¾″, (Metropolitan Museum of Art, N.Y., David Hunter McAlpin Fund.)

to get rid of its prim nursery look. No wonder those old photographs of us, leaning over imaginary ramparts of heaven, look anxious and wistful. This is how we felt . . .[3]

Cameron's feelings for beauty and nature explode in rich images. Although the emotion reflected on the sitter's features might have resulted from the strain of hours of posing for the demanding photographer, Cameron's intensity and her commitment to the image she was creating were communicated to her sitter. He or she was never allowed to forget the transcendent importance of this experience to the photographer. William Allingham related this incident in his diary:

> June 10, 1867—Down train comes in with Mrs. Cameron, queenly in carriage by herself, surrounded by photographs. We go by Lymington together, she talking all the time. "I want to do a large portrait of Tennyson and he objects! Says I make bags under his eyes—and Carlyle refuses to give me a sitting, he says it is a kind of inferno. The greatest men of the age (with strong emphasis) Sir John Herschel, Henry Taylor, Watts, say I have immortalised them, and these men object!"[4]

The persistent Mrs. Cameron got her way—along with Tennyson and Carlyle she photographed Holman Hunt, Darwin, Longfellow, Robert Browning, Ellen Terry, and countless sons and daughters of friends, as well as many of the servants and local inhabitants of Freshwater.

Cameron was an artist about whom legends grew, if only because her manner and speech and her passionate enthusiasm made her an eccentric in the period in which she lived. The story is told that one model, Kate Shepard, was discovered by Cameron while begging on the road, rescued by the magnanimous photographer, and pressed into service as parlormaid, and of course, model. It was believed that as the ugly duckling among the beautiful Pattle sisters, Cameron sought to create through photography the beauty she herself did not possess. She would go to any lengths for a beautiful image, including kicking her camera stand during a long exposure to throw the image out of focus and soften the harsh reality of her sitter's human flaws—and insisting that her sitter's hair be washed and let dry uncombed. The portraits that resulted are a strange blend of sentiment and art, for they combine the photographer's enthusiastic expectations of what a great man should look like, with strong, pure, compositional interpretation that does more to give import to the subject than costume or soft tones. Cameron's intentions are best summed up in her own words:

> At last yesterday I achieved the picture with as much power and pathos as one can bring into a photograph consistently with what I think the great principle of high art—reserve and composure, expressive of subdued passion . . .[5]

Lewis Carroll, in a letter to his sister written in 1864, gave Julia Cameron's photographs a mixed review:

> In the evening, Mrs. Cameron and I had a mutual exhibition of photographs. Hers are all taken purposely out of focus—some are very picturesque—some merely hideous—however she talks about them as if they were triumphs of art.[6]

Carroll became interested in photography in 1855, while a mathematics lecturer at Christ Church, Oxford. Within a year he had taken his first successful pictures. He became incurably addicted to pursuing famous personalities, especially aristocrats, in hopes of persuading them to sit for him. Unlike Cameron, Carroll concentrated on making an attractively composed likeness of his sitter, not capturing some internal spiritual quality. He rarely deviated from a standard format—full-figure, careful use of empty space, and an arrangement of props. Although his portraits of such notables as Rosetti (Figure 72), Faraday and Millais are executed with skill, most lack the special quality of intimacy that distinguishes his portraits of children.

As a photographer of little girls, Carroll remains unsurpassed. His greatest joy—and principle hobby—was entertaining the young daughters of his friends and colleagues. Photography sessions became another of the games Carroll amused the children with.[7] In his study in Christ Church, he kept a vast collection of toys, dolls, music boxes, stuffed animals, puzzles, and playthings he had designed himself, including a wind-up toy bear and a bat that could fly around the room. He also kept a collection of fancy dresses, trimmed in lace, for the girls to pose in, and he never tired of telling stories or drawing silly pictures to the delight of the children. When he sensed that his little friends were most happy and relaxed, Carroll would produce his camera, made ready beforehand, and the portraits that resulted are a rare collection of personal, natural, and tender reflections of his feelings.

Carroll's portraits of little girls are deceptively simple in style. Most often

Figure 72. D. Gabriel Rossetti, by Lewis Carroll, October 6, 1863, 4 × 5½ (Gernsheim Collection, Humanities Research Center, University of Texas, Austin).

Figure 73. Alice Liddell (later Mrs. Reginald Hargreaves), for whom "Alices Adventures Underground" was written, by Lewis Carroll, c. 1859. (Capt. Caryle Hargreaves, Gernsheim Collection, Humanities Research Center, University of Texas, Austin). Carroll included this portrait in the original book of *Alice In Wonderland*.

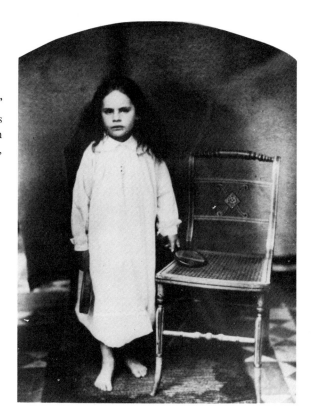

Figure 74. "It won't come smooth . . ." Portrait of Irene MacDonald by Lewis Carroll, July, 1863, 6″ × 8″. (Gernsheim Collection, Humanities Research Center, University of Texas, Austin)

Figure 75. Agnes Grace Weld as Little Red Ridinghood, by Lewis Carroll, 1852, 5½″ × 3¾″. This and another photograph were Lewis Carroll's means of introduction to Tennyson. (Gernsheim Collection, Humanities Research Center, University of Texas, Austin).

Figure 76. Beatrice Henley, by Lewis Carroll, September, 1862 at Putney, 3¾″ × 5¼″. (Gernsheim Collection, Humanities Research Center, University of Texas, Austin)

Figure 77. Florence Bickersteth by Lewis Carroll, taken on September 8, 1865, 5″ × 7″. (Gernsheim Collection, Humanities Research Center, University of Texas, Austin)

he poses them outdoors, sitting on steps, leaning against a tree trunk, in front of a stone fence or brick wall. His indoor portraits are usually simple too—the girls are seated more times than not, in a chair or in a corner of a room. The striking similarity among his portraits is in the naturalness of expression. There is never the appearance of contrivance, and in almost every case, the child's expression seems startlingly intimate. One portrait, entitled *It Won't Come Smooth* (Figure 74), showing Irene Macdonald in the process of trying to brush her hair, escapes sentimentality in spite of the title and subject matter because of the child's sensual expression, full-lipped and intense, and her natural pose, with her left foot curled slightly on the carpet. The same holds true with the portrait of Agnes Grace Weld, as Little Red Ridinghood (Figure 75). Carroll has taken a conventional genre subject and made an image filled with emotional tension—the wide-eyed and mysterious expression on the girl's face and her graceful pose, in combination with the texture of the cloak and the pattern of leaves behind her, elevate the subject beyond the fairytale. These portraits are charmingly natural: In the portrait of Beatrice Henley (Figure 76), the subject, who is smiling slightly to herself at some special personal secret, stands holding a straw hat, her feet casually crossed in their high button shoes. Florence Bickersteth (Figure 77) leans wistfully out of a window, her hands gracefully placed in front of her, with an expression that allows the viewer to believe he is the witness to a private moment of daydream or fantasy. In each study, the pose and expression are inextricably bound, so that each portrait is as unique as Carroll's sense of the individual child.

Carroll's portraits of little girls are sometimes viewed with disapproval, especially since he often photographed the girls naked. He wrote to one mother in explanation:

> If I had the loveliest child in the world, to draw or photograph, and found she had a modest shrinking (however slight and however easily overcome) from being taken in the nude, I should feel it was a solemn duty owed to God to drop the request altogether.[8]

In fact, he requested, that in case these nude portraits embarrass the girls, the negative plates be destroyed after his death. His photographs are the expression of a particular passion, and in his ability to transfer his repressed feelings into the photographic image, he was almost alone among his Victorian contemporaries. Since Carroll we have seen other photographs—Stieglitz' portraits of Georgia O'Keeffe for example—that make use of the same physical and emotional energy to create a portrait, but Carroll was one of the first, and one of the most special. The portraits that remain intact are not sordid or obscene, but an extraordinary glimpse into the spirit of children, brought to the height of childish enthusiasm by this staid and rather serious mathematics lecturer.

The stylistic and conceptual differences between the photographs of Cameron and Carroll can be better understood by a comparison of portraits they each made of Alfred Lord Tennyson. Tennyson was Cameron's friend, so conceivably it might have been easier for her to take liberties with her sitter not permitted other photographers—although from the vivid descriptions we have of Cameron's determination, probably she would have taken similar liberties with a stranger. Lewis Carroll, however, stood in awe of famous men. We learn from his journals that he waited patiently, and planned with the keenness of a general, his campaign to request permission to photograph the celebrated poet. His portrait (Figure 79) shows the full figure of a man, seated rather stiffly, in a chair, wearing a cape and broad-brimmed hat. One of Tennyson's hands is obscured by his cape, while the other is stiff, unnaturally held. A bland facial expression adds little to this somewhat theatrical pose, so that we receive almost no information about Tennyson's character, except that this is a man who seems to take himself very seriously. More likely, the photographer was determined to make Tennyson look like his idea of Poet Laureate. Carroll photographed Tennyson on several other occasions, at Farringford, Tennyson's home in Freshwater, and at Coniston, in the Lake District, where Tennyson stayed for summer holidays. On one of these occasions he expressed disappointment about the poet's appearance in his journal: "A strange, shaggy-looking man; his hair mustache and beard looked wild and neglected; these very much hid the character of the face. . . ."[9] This time Carroll chose to photograph Tennyson in a contrived studious pose and costume, with a result which is almost comical in its stiffness and air of studied sobriety.

Cameron, in her famous portrait, which Tennyson dubbed *The Dirty Monk* (Figure 78), did all but starve the poet to achieve her character interpretation. Tennyson was posed in a monk's robe with tousled hair (in the Cameron style). The composition is striking—Tennyson's hand clasping a book in the lower right-hand corner of the photograph duplicates the triangular shape of the central figure, so that the repetition of shapes leads the eye directly to the face and strong profile of the man. Since Cameron insisted that soft focus lent a spiritual quality to the portrait, most important details of character in the face are obscured, and we are left with only the clues Cameron provides, the book,

I prefer the dirty monk
to the others of me

A Tennyson

except me by Mayall

Figure 79. Portrait of Tennyson, by Lewis Carroll. (Courtesy of Weston Naef)

Figure 80. Portrait of Tennyson, by John J. E. Mayall. (Courtesy of Weston Naef)

Figure 78. (*opposite*) Portrait of Tennyson, by Julia Margaret Cameron, 1865. 7¼″ × 9″. This portrait, which Tennyson called "The Dirty Monk" was used as the frontispiece for *Idylls of the King*, Vol. I. (Metropolitan Museum of Art, N.Y.)

the costume, and the poet's messy appearance, to determine the personality of the man. Cameron defines her approach to this portrait by saying, "it is a fit representation of Isaiah or Jeremiah," which may well be true! The viewer who did not know the sitter was Tennyson would be hard pressed to establish where this holy man belonged in the scheme of things. Although Cameron cheerfully omits worldly details from her portrait, it is far from a failure. She has portrayed Tennyson as she herself feels about him, rather than as society sees him. Tennyson's friend F. D. Maurice wrote to Cameron about her portrait of the poet:

> Had we such portraits of Shakespeare and of Milton, we should have better commentaries on Hamlet and Comus than we now possess, even as you have secured to us a better commentary on "Maud" and "In Memoriam" than all our critics have ever given us or will give us.[10]

Tennyson himself preferred a portrait taken, not by Carroll or Cameron, but by J. J. Mayall, the same photographer who was the "oddest man" Queen Victoria ever saw (Figure 80). The Mayall portrait of Tennyson is a semiprofile head-shot, similar to Cameron's but with penetrating, exquisite detail. Tennyson's strong profile is emphasized, not so much by composition, as in the Cameron portrait, but by a softening in detail on one side of the face, while the other side is rendered with immaculate clarity. The details that the photographer has recorded, the beautiful tones in the folds of skin on the poet's cheek, the slight balding and carelessly combed hair, provide us with clues about the man's personality. There is a sense of power and authority in the fleshy molding of the face, and the repeated shift from sharp to soft focus enhances the forceful expression. Mayall created a portrait of a determined yet sensitive man, but above all, a man who has experienced life fully. One can easily understand why Tennyson felt more comfortable with Mayall's portrait than with Cameron's rather grandiose vision.

From all three photographs of Tennyson we can make certain assumptions about the relationship between a portrait photographer and his sitter. We can see from Carroll's portrait of Tennyson, that a photographer may be dominated by his sitter, or influenced by a pre-conceived idea. The resulting portraits are usually dull, without the benefit of the skilled photographer's visual editing. Another possibility is that the photographer's personal feeling may be the controlling factor in a portrait's creation, rather than the sitter's personality. These portraits, like Cameron's, are not accurate as historical documents, except in terms of the individual impressions of the photographer who recorded them. Oftentimes these are the most valuable portraits because we learn as much about the photographer as about the sitter. Mayall's portrait follows the pattern of many portraits of famous men and women, in that the photographer relies on realistic rendering of details about the sitter, enhanced and interpreted by skillful use of photographic tones. Portraits of this type are deceptive, because they seem to be accurate documents of the personality of the sitter—actually they result from a process of subtle selectivity exercised by the photographer, so that the viewer's attention is drawn to the specific aspects of the sitter that the photographer wished to emphasize. The main distinction between Cameron's approach to portraiture and Mayall's is that Cameron presents her fantasy about the sitter by the clues she adds to the portrait, while Mayall edits details about the sitter to achieve his character interpretation.

The portraits of another fine Victorian photographer, Dr. Hugh Welch Diamond, represent the first body of work to link photographic portraiture to psychology. Dr. Diamond was appointed superintendent of the women's division of Surrey County Asylum in 1848, about the time he became actively interested in photography. As a founding member and secretary of the Photographic Society, Diamond was closely involved with the community of serious photographers in London. When he decided to specialize in mental illness, Diamond began to record with his camera the faces and expressions of his patients, in the hope that these isolated images would give him clues to the workings of their minds and facilitate his treatment of them. The collection of photographs, all of women, are a bizarre and affecting representation of lives that have gone out of control. The stillness of the calotype and the softness of the diffused image provide a strangely inappropriate quality to the portraits, in contrast with the harsh realism of the emotions which are so close to the surface (Figure 81). Dr. Diamond confronts each of his sitters, women who by nature of their illnesses had been isolated from the world, and makes their experiences public. As viewers we too confront these people, their lunacy apparent in their distorted expressions and lack of focus, made vital by the unyielding accuracy of Diamond's fine prints. Some of the faces that were recorded have a childlike simplicity, but more often the expressions reflect an inner world that these women were unable to hide behind a public facade. Dr. Diamond wrote of his experiment:

> The photographer catches in a moment the permanent cloud, or the passing storm or sunshine of the soul, and thus enables the metaphysician to witness

Figure 81. Mental patients, Surrey County Asylum, by Dr. Hugh Welch Diamond. (Royal Photographic Society, London)

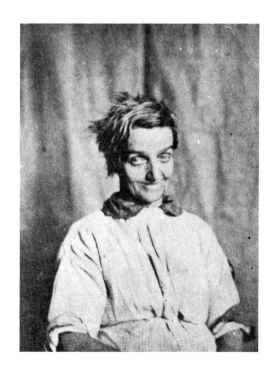

and trace out the connection between the visible and the invisible in one important branch of his researches into the philosophy of the human mind.[11]

That Dr. Diamond's portraits still carry an impact for the modern viewer who has been over-exposed to documentary photography testifies to the integrity of the photographer, whose interest was treatment and cure at best, and understanding at all times, rather than sensation or novelty.

Oscar Gustave Rejlander also experimented with recording his sitter's emotions, but his career as a photographer was less cohesive than Diamond's— Rejlander seems to have been less interested in science than in personal publicity and financial success. He was born in Sweden and came to England after marrying an English woman. Originally a portrait painter, he gave up painting but continued to imitate painters with his camera. Rejlander's technique was to combine many negatives to create one scene, usually with an allegorical theme. His most famous, *The Two Ways Of Life,* took thirty negatives to complete, and the rumor of the day was that Rejlander employed over twenty nude models. Rejlander's best photographs were his portraits— when he was able to overcome his predilection for sentimentality and trite imagery. To the horror of his fellow photographers, Rejlander insisted that if all the light which had no part in the portrait he was making was shut out, the image would be more forceful. He set his camera in a "dark, tapering passage" with spot-lighting (a term then unknown) coming from the top and side. His portrait of Gustave Doré (Figure 82), taken in 1860, shows the famous French illustrator languidly reclining on a chaise-longue, with an indolent expression to match his pose, exactly as if caught unaware by the camera. Doré was enthusiastic about the portrait, which was in fact carefully posed, but critics were scandalized by Rejlander's rejection of the formal style of posed portrait. His other portraits using "concentrated daylight" looked like candid pictures; although these were a foretaste of the portrait style to dominate photography in the next century, Rejlander's portraits were considered technically poor by his contemporaries who preferred such whimsical creations as his *What Ails Amy?* and *Is it True?* or *Did She?*

During a period when Rejlander was desperate for money, he was prevailed upon by Charles Darwin to illustrate his book *The Expression of Emotions In Man and Animals.* While some of these photographs are contrived, others show the perceptive eye of the photographer, and his understanding of Darwin's

Figure 82. Gustave Doré, by O. J. Rejlander. (Royal Photographic
Society, London)

Portraits by O. J. Rejlander for Charles Darwin's
Expression of the Emotions in Man and Animals

Figure 83. "Disdain."

Figure 84. "Uncovering the canine tooth."

Figure 85. "Infant crying."

experiment. Darwin wrote about the photograph *Sneering and Defiance* (Figure 84):

> Mr. Rejlander, without my having made any illusion to the subject, asked me whether I had ever noticed this expression as he had been much struck by it. He has photographed for me a lady, who sometimes unintentionally displays the canine on one side, and who can do so voluntarily with unusual distinction.[12]

Other expressions recorded by the photographer were *Weeping, Smiling, Helplessness, Disgust, Surprise, Indignation,* and many more. To illustrate *Mental Distress,* Rejlander photographed a wailing child, and the picture became a huge success. Finally Rejlander received the critical acclaim he wanted, as sixty thousand copies and more cartes-de-visites of "Jinxes Baby" were sold. Ironically, Rejlander's daylight portraits, his candid and natural character studies, were among the most sophisticated portrait photographs of the period, but he is remembered chiefly for his portraits of a howling child and allegorical cartoons made with many negatives and seminude figures.

We know very little about Lady Hawarden's reasons for learning photography, except to assume that as the wife of the fourth Viscount Hawarden Cornwallis Maud, she was not motivated by the promise of financial reward. Lady Hawarden worked quietly in her London townhouse, without much contact with other photographers. Her photographs are enhanced by natural light from the tall windows of her mansion, so that they glow with diffused sunlight and rich shadows. Unlike Julia Cameron, Lady Hawarden never made close-up portraits, preferring to include the drapery and flowing clothing of the period as part of the compositional whole. Many of her portraits were of children and young girls, photographed bending over balconies, seated reading in late afternoon shadows, sewing, or whispering confidentially to friends (Figure 86). Her portraits have a special charm, in the romantic tranquility of the Victorian settings, which remind us of billowing skirts, elegant rooms, and the genteel life of young girls in high button shoes and crinolines.

The nominal content of Lady Hawarden's portraits, however, is less significant than the composition and form, for no other Victorian photographer was as skilled in using structure and line, shadow and highlight to enrich the construction of a picture. Lady Hawarden was influenced by the Pre-Raphaelite movement, and her photographs show an awareness, scarcely shared by her contemporaries, that composition is an aspect of the image, rather than the defining element of the picture. Lady Hawarden joined the Royal Photographic Society in 1863, where she received many prizes for her

Figure 86. Young girls, by Countess Hawarden. (Victoria and Albert
Museum, London)

photographs; her promising career was cut short by her death, six months later, at the age of 41.

All the photographers mentioned so far have achieved some measure of recognition in the anthologies and in museums and galleries. There remains a body of portrait photography produced by amateurs that has virtually been ignored. One reason is that rarely has a portfolio been preserved intact, unless the photographer made provision in his will for his pictures to be preserved as a group. Usually photographs were scattered among family and friends or were destroyed; in some cases, museums have full collections of Victorian photographs tucked in the backrooms of archives, waiting to be uncovered and catalogued, as was the case with the Hill and Adamson albums from the Royal Academy. One such album of portraits, by an amateur calotypist named William Collie, was discovered in the basement of the Royal Photographic Society in London—portraits of a surprisingly fine quality both in terms of craftsmanship and content.[13] Collie received practically no recognition during his lifetime, except for a brief mention of his portraits in the catalogue of the Great Exhibition, and his photographs have never been exhibited publicly in this century.[14] These photographs provide a rare oportunity for unprejudiced viewing and criticism and may serve as a reminder that much Victorian photography still in existence has yet to be brought to light.

William Collie, a portrait painter and professor of drawing in Jersey, in the Channel Islands, began to experiment with the calotype process in the spring of 1847. Collie was not a professional photographer; at least the British Press Almanac, which was the local directory, made no mention of Collie, nor did Thomas Sutton's journal *Photographic Notes*, published on the island. Collie concentrated on photographing the local inhabitants of Jersey, probably intending at first to use the calotype process to record subject matter for the portraits he painted. Looking at the body of Collie's work, it becomes clear, by his repeated attempts at portraying certain individuals or groups of people, by changes in his interpretation of character and atmosphere, that Collie began to regard the calotype portrait as an end in itself.

Collie's portrait of a girl with a washbucket (Figure 87), is a compelling photograph, remarkable for the simplicity with which he captures the beauty of this working girl in her plain clothing. Within the boundaries of the picture frame lies a composition of elegant design and strong lines. Collie used ordinary objects, the fence the girl leans on and her wooden washbucket, as props to direct the eye into the picture. Soft, warm, gray tones, suggestive of light and shade, conceal the background just enough to alter the picture from documentary realism to a more personal vision. The girl's expression, which is

Figure 87. (*opposite*) Girl with a washbucket.

Calotype portraits, by William Collie (Taken in Jersey, Channel Islands, c. 1844). (Royal Photographic Society, London)

Figure 88. Man, age 102, and his great-great grandchild.

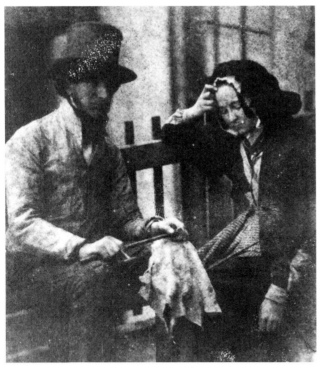

Figure 89. Man and woman.

Figure 90. Woman with baskets of vegetables.

Figure 91. Woman knitting.

tranquil without being sad, invites speculation about her thoughts and her dreams, and this special mood is enhanced by the exquisite pose of her head as she leans on her hand, by the subtle shadow at the side of her face and the luminous pearly tones of her skin. The undefined background makes it difficult to determine if the girl stands against a wall or is surrounded by empty space, adding another dimension to the picture. The space within the picture frame becomes a total environment, unified by softly shifting gray tones. The girl and her thoughts belong to the environment of the photograph, rather than to the harsher workday world her clothes would suggest.

In another portrait, Collie's subjects are an old man, aged 102, and his great-great-grandchild (Figure 88). Collie appears to have been the silent witness to an intimate moment in the lives of two people. One cannot say whether the old man is clinging to the child, or if the reverse is true, because their arms are interlocked and their bodies lean toward each other. The eye goes from the old man's face, grimacing slightly in the sun, to the child's soft, pouting face, pressed close to the old man's arm, and to the two pairs of hands, side by side. In spite of the contrast between the old man's age and experience and the child's tender innocence, the two individuals are compositionally united so that they form one central figure, each dependent on the other. Collie dealt with youth and old age with an almost Tolstoyan understanding of human relationships. The photograph is about trust and need and was made with artless honesty.

Collie's photographs probably have a different meaning from the actual situation he was recording. Perhaps the couple in Figure 89 happened to be seated together as Collie passed with his camera. Most likely, the woman's head was bowed to avoid the sun, and she leaned on the fence to steady herself. Whatever the history of the situation, Collie's portrait suggests an unspoken bond between two people. The woman's position is open and vulnerable, with her arms spread apart and her head bent. The man sits erect with his fist clenched and his body leaning forward, as if to protect the woman. Their knees appear to be touching, although we are not certain because the cloth obscures our view, but the shadow behind the man and the reflected cross pattern behind the woman push the people together within the enclosed space of the photograph. The result is an intimate atmosphere, enriched with light and shadow, which seems to isolate these two people from the rest of the world. Here Collie speaks of companionship, with insight and compassion.

William Collie's photographs are outstanding because of the control and careful organization he brought to each image. His portfolio includes a number of photographs of the same subject, taken over a period of years. We can see that Collie used each calotype image of the same subject to work progressively toward the finished product. His photographs of people include many categories—people at work, a man painting, gypsy women, chess players, a guitar player, local women selling vegetables or knitting (Figures 90 and 91), and a selection pictures which explore relationships between two or more people. Collie brought a painter's eye and a draftsman's discipline to photography, with the result that he used the camera to make memorable pictures rather than authentic documents.

Victorian portrait photography travelled a fine line between fact and fiction. Many amateur portraits were genre photographs, dependent on a strong fictional story line usually with a moral, and executed in a formal, composed, and painterly manner. In these pictures, the photographer was evidently the organizer, and the image resulted from the mechanical execution of a literal idea. Another type of popular amateur photography was pure documentation. The camera made it easy for the photographer to remain neutral, so that his or her presence did not intrude on the scene, or object, or sitter any more than was necessary. The camera was often used as a diversion or out of a desire for recording one's life, and the only difference between amateurs then and snapshooters now, except in rare cases, was the greater effort required to get a picture. Since recreational photography was not regarded with the reverence of "art" photography, very few of these amateur photographs were carefully preserved.

The best of the work by Victorian amateurs derives strength from a subtle blend of fact and fiction. These photographs—and this is true with respect to Collie as well as Cameron—are less involved with art than with an objective rendering of human relationships and a genuine concern with the quality of their sitter's lives.

Notes

1. Helmut Gernsheim, *Julia Margaret Cameron: Her Life and Photographic Work,* Fountain Press, London, 1948, p. 16.

2. From *Annals of My Glasshouse,* quoted in *ibid., p. 21.*

3. *Ibid, p. 22.*

4. *Ibid.,* p. 25.

5. Brian Hill, *Julia Margaret Cameron, A Victorian Family Portrait,* St. Martin's Press, N.Y., 1973, p. 83.

6. Helmut Gernsheim, *Lewis Carroll: Photographer,* Max Parrish and Co. Ltd., London, 1949, p. 55.

7. Mrs. Reginald Hargreaves (the former Alice Liddell) remembers: "Being photographed was a joy to us, and not a penance as it is to most children," when asked about Carroll's photography.

8. Lewis Carroll, *The Annotated Alice,* Clarkson N. Potter, New York, 1960, p. 11.

9. Helmut Gernsheim, *Lewis Carroll: Photographer,* Max Parrish and Co., Ltd., London, 1949, p. 90.

10. *Alfred Lord Tennyson And His Friends,* a Series of 25 Portraits and a Frontispiece in Photogravure, from the Negatives of Mrs. J. M. Cameron, and H. H. H. Cameron, London 1893, Metropolitan Museum of Art, N.Y.—from a letter written to Mrs. Cameron by F. D. Maurice, in 1866.

11. *Photographic Journal,* May 1856.

12. Charles Darwin, *The Expression Of The Emotions In Man And Animals,* London, 1873, p. 250.

13. Listed in *Photographic Journal,* March 1937, p. 172, under *Gifts,* was, "A volume of calotypes, circa 1847, by William Collie, a portrait painter and photographer, from his grand-niece Mrs. A. Marett per Mr. Emile F. Greiton, for the permanent collection of the Royal Photographic Society, London."

14. "Great Exhibition Catalogue," Vol. II, p. 941 22: "Collie, William, Belmont House, St. Helier, Jersey, Producer, Calotype Pictures From Life—'French and Jersey Market Women' . . .The peculiar brilliancy of the atmosphere of these islands, combined with the balance of blue light reflected from the sea, was found by the writer to communicate an almost instantaneous impression to paper or plates. . ."

Bibliography

History of Photography

Beaton, Cecil, and Buckland, Gail. *The Magic Image*. Boston: Little Brown & Company, 1975.

Braive, Michel François. *The Era of the Photograph: A Social History* (translated by D. Britt). London: Thames and Hudson, 1966.

Eder, Josef Maria. *The History of Photography* (translated by Edward Epstean). New York: Columbia University Press, 1945.

Focal Encyclopedia of Photography. London: The Focal Press, 1956.

Gernsheim, Helmut, and Gernsheim, Alison. *The History of Photography from the Earliest Use of the Camera Obscura in the Eleventh Century Up to 1914*. New York: Oxford University Press, 1955.

Gernsheim, Helmut. *Masterpieces of Victorian Photography*. London: Phaidon Press, 1951.

Newhall, Beaumont. *The History of Photography from 1939 to the Present Day*. New York: Museum of Modern Art in collaboration with George Eastman House, 1964.

Pollack, Peter. *The Picture History of Photography from the Earliest Beginnings to the Present Day*. New York: Harry N. Abrams, 1958.

Strasser, Alex. *Immortal Portraits. Being a gallery of famous photographs by David Octavius Hill, Julia Margaret Cameron, Roger Fenton and others*. London: The Focal Press, 1941.

Sutton, Thomas. *The Calotype Process*. London: Joseph Cundall, 1855.

Taft, Robert. *Photography and the American Scene*. New York: Dover Press, 1938.

Individual Photographers

ARCHER, FREDERICK SCOTT

———. *The Chemist,* March 1851. The first practical collodion process. A revised and enlarged text was published by Archer in *Photography and Fine Arts Journal* 7 (1854): 112–117.

———. "Frederick Scott Archer, Biography," *British Journal of Photography* 22: 102–104, Feb. 26, 1875. See also Harrison's *History of Photography,* 1887, p. 39–40.

BEARD, RICHARD

———. English patent no. 8546, June 13, 1840.
———. English patent no. 9292, March 10, 1842.
  Claims on camera using concave mirrors instead of a lens, also the use of head rest and lighting apparatus to control illumination for portraits, a method of burnishing the silver surface of the plate, and the use of bromine or bromic acid in sensitizing the plate.

Mayhew, Henry. *London Labour and the London Poor: The Condition and Earnings of Those That Will Work, Cannot Work, and Will Not Work,* 3 vols. London: Charles Griffen & Co., 1851–1865.
  Illustrated with wood engravings (from photographs credited to Beard).

CAMERON, JULIA MARGARET

———. "Annals of My Glass House." *Photographic Journal* 67: 296–301. July 1927.

———. Illustrations to Tennyson's *Idylls of the King and Other Poems.* Large folio. London: H. S. King, 1875.
  Frontispiece: mounted photographic portrait of Tennyson; 12 mounted photographs illustrating the text with Cameron's hand-written, dated, signed, and underlined titles. Text in facsimile handwriting with facsimile of Tennyson's signature.

———. Cameron, H. H. H. *Alfred Lord Tennyson and His Friends: A Series of 25 Portraits and Frontispiece in Photogravure from the Negatives of Mrs. J. M. Cameron and H. H. H. Cameron, with Reminiscences by Anee Thackeray Ritchie.* London, 1893.

Fry, Roger, and Woolf, Virginia. *Victorian Photographs of Famous Men and Fair Women.* London: Hogarth Press, 1926.

Gernsheim, Helmut. *Julia Margaret Cameron.* London: Fountain Press, 1948.

Schwarz, Heinrich. *Julia Margaret Cameron.* Complete Phot. No. 10, p. 593–595, illus.

CARROLL, LEWIS (Pseudonym of Charles Lutwidge Dodgson)

Gernsheim, Helmut: *Lewis Carroll, Photographer*. London, 1949.

CLAUDET, ANTOINE JEAN FRANÇOIS

————. English patent no. 9193, December 18, 1841.
   The most interesting claims of this patent are for the use of artificial light for night portraiture, and for the use of colored light, preferably red, in the processing room.

————. English patent no. 9957, November 21, 1843.
   Process for converting daguerreotype into a printing plate.

Ellis, J. *Claudet, A., F.R.S.A., Memoir*, 1868.
————. *Récherches sur les principaux phenomènes de la photographie*. Paris: Lerebours, 1850.

Claudet, A., *Du stéréoscope et de ses applications à la photographie*. Paris: Lerebour et Secretan, 1853.

Colas, F. *Derniers perfectionnements apportés au daguerreotype*. Paris: Lerebours et Secretan, 1853.

Gill, Arthur T. "Antoine François Jean Claudet (1797–1867)." *Photographic Journal* 107: (December 1967): 405–408.

COLLIE, WILLIAM

————. A volume of calotypes, c. 1847 [permanent collection of the Royal Photographic Society, London]. Listed in *Photographic Journal* (March 1837): p. 172 under 'Gifts.'
————. *Great Exhibition Catalogue*, Vol. 2 p. 941: "Calotype Pictures from Life— 'French and Jersey Market Women.'"

DAGUERRE, LOUIS JACQUES MANDÉ

————. English patent no. 8194 (with Joseph Isidore Niépce Jr.), August 14, 1839. Issued to Miles Berry.

————. "Historique et description des procédés du daguerréotype et du diorama," par Daguerre, Peintre, inventeur du Diorama, officier de la Légion-d'Honneur, membre de plusieurs Académies, etc., Paris. Alphonse Giroux et Cie, Rue du Coq-Saint-Honoré, 7 Ou se fabriquent les Appareils, Delloye, Libraire, Place de la Bourse, 13. 1839." (Published on or about 20 August. Not listed in the Bibliographie de la France.) Printed by Bethune et Plon.

————. "History and process of photogenic drawing by means of the Daguerreotype. Published by order of the French Government." With notes and illustrated by six engravings. London: William Strange, 21, Paternoster Row. Printed by R. MacDonald. (British Museum copy dated 19 October.)

Eder, Joseph Maria. *History of Photography,* pp. 207–257. New York: 1945.

Gernsheim, Helmut, and Gernsheim Alison. *L. J. M. Daguerre: The History of the Diorama and the Daguerreotype.* New York: Dover Publications, 1969.

Newhall, Beaumont. "Monsieur Daguerre, His Life and Work," *Modern Photography,* December 1951, p. 74; January 1952, p. 76.

Potonniee, George. *History of the Discovery of Photography*, Chaps. 27–32, pp. 146–182. New York, 1936.

FENTON, ROGER

Gernsheim, Helmut, and Gernsheim, Alison *Roger Fenton, Photographer of the Crimean War.* London, 1958.

Gill, Arthur T. "One Hundred Years Ago," *Photographic Journal* 109 (August 1969): 484–485. [Obit and portrait and biographical notes on Roger Fenton.)

HILL, DAVID OCTAVIUS and ADAMSON, ROBERT

———. Calotypes illustrating an early stage in the development of photography. Selected from his collection by Andrew Elliot. Folio, Edinburgh, 1928. 47 calotype portraits from the original negatives.

Nickel, Heinrick. *David Octavius Hill.* Halle, 1960.

Major, A. Hyatt. "The First Victorian Photographer," *Metropolitan Museum of Art Bulletin.* December 1958.

Michaelson, Katherine. *A centenary Exhibition of the work of David Octavius Hill and Robert Adamson.* Edinburgh, 1970.

Schwarz, Heinrich. *David Octavius Hill, Master of Photography* (translated from the German by Helene E. Fraenkel). New York: Viking, 1931.

NIÉPCE, NICÉPHORE

———. "Notice sur l'Héliographie" in L. J. M. Daguerre, *Historique et description des procédés du Daguerréotype*, Paris, 1839.

Vigneau, Andre. *Une breve histoire de l'art de Niepce a nos jours.* Paris, 1963.

SILVY, CAMILLE DA

————. *Daybooks* (permanent collection, National Portrait Gallery, London) c. 1860.

TALBOT, WILLIAM HENRY FOX

————. English patent no. 8842, February 8, 1841.
The fourth, fifth and sixth parts of this patent (disclaimed by Talbot March 8, 1854) apply to coloring daguerreotypes in a lead solution, obtaining very thin daguerreotype plates, and printing on daguerreotypes through paper negatives.

————. "Some Account of the Art of Photogenic Drawing, or the Process by which Natural Objects may be made to Delineate Themselves without the aid of the Artist's Pencil." *Proceedings Royal Society* 4, 1839, p. 120–121; *Phil. Mag.* 14, 1839, p. 196–211. Read before the Royal Society, January 31, 1839. Reprinted separately by R. and J. E. Taylor, London, 1839.

————. "Photogenic Drawings," *The Mechanics' Journal of Science and Art,* February 16 and 23, 1839.
This gives the text of the paper Talbot presented at the Royal Institution on January 31, 1839, constituting the first disclosure of the negative-positive process with light-sensitive silver salts which initiated the modern photographic process.

————. *The pencil of nature.* London: Longman, Brown, Green and Longmans, 1844.

Epstean, Edward. *William Henry Fox Talbot.* New York, 1934.

Gernsheim, Helmut. "Talbot's and Herschel's Photographic Experiments in 1839," *Image* 8 (1959): 132–137.

Gill, Arthur T. "Another Look at Fox Talbot's '1839' Camera," *Photographic Journal* 106 (October 1966): 344–345.

Newhall, Beaumont. "William Henry Fox Talbot," *Image* 8 (1959): 60–75.

Talbot, M. T. "The Life and Personality of Fox Talbot," *Photographic Journal* 79 (1939): 546–549; *J. Roy. Soc. Arts* 87: 826–830, June 23, 1939.

Thomas, D. B. *The First Negatives: An Account of the Discovery and Early Use of the Negative-Positive Photographic Process* (a Science Museum monograph). London: H. M. Stationery Office, 1964.

Snow, V. F., and Thomas, D. B. "The Talbotype Establishment at Reading—1844 to 1847." *Photographic Journal* 106 (February 1966): 56–67.

WILSON, GEORGE WASHINGTON

Peterich, Gerda. "G. W. W. The Instantaneous Photography of a Photographer of Queen Victoria's Time, George Washington Wilson." *Image* 5 (December 1956): 220–229.

WOLCOTT, ALEXANDER SIMON

——. English patent no. 9672 (with John Johnson), March 18, 1843.

Illustrated Books

Darwin, Charles. *The Expression of the Emotions in Man and Animals* (with photographs by Oscar Gustave Rejlander). London, 1873.

Elliot, Andrew. *Calotypes by D. O. Hill and Robert Adamson.* Edinburgh, 1928. [See Hill, David Octavius]

Fry, Herbert. *Photographic Portraits of Living Celebrities.* No. 1 Professor Owen, London, 1856.
   Biographical notice of Sir Richard Owen by Herbert Fry, illustrated with a photographic portrait by Maull & Polyblank.

Mayhew, Henry. *London Labour and the London Poor,* London, 1851–65. Illustrated with wood engravings (from photographs by Richard Beard). [See Beard, Richard]

Photographic Historical Portrait Gallery, consisting of a Series of Portraits, principally from Miniatures in the most celebrated Collections in England. Photographed by L. Caldesi & Co., London, P. and A. Colnaghi, Scott & Co., 1864. 50 photographic plates.

Reeve, Lovell. *Portraits of Men of Eminence in Literature, Science and Art, with Biographical Memoirs.* The Photographs from Life, by Ernest Edwards. 6 vols. London: Reeve & Co., 1863. With 144 photographic portraits.

Talbot, W. H. F. *The Pencil of Nature.* London, Longman, Brown, Green and Longmans, 1844. 80 p, 24 photographs. [Libr. of Congr.] [NYPL] [RPS] [Grap. Lehr.] [See Talbot, William Henry Fox]

Tennyson, Alfred Lord. *Idylls of the King and other poems* with illustrative photographs by Julia Margaret Cameron. Large Folio. London, 1875. [See Cameron, Julia Margaret]

Tennyson, Alfred Lord. *Idylls of the King and other poems.* Miniature Edition. London, 1875. Contains 23 photographs by Julia Margaret Cameron.

Victoria, Queen. *Leaves from a Journal of Our Life in the Highlands from 1848 to 1861*. Edited by Arthur Helps. Illustrated with 42 photographs. London, 1868.

Related Works

Beal, S. B. *Carte-de-visite portraits of the Royal Family, Eminent and Celebrated Persons*. London, 1866.

Bennett, A. R. *London and Londoners in the 1850's and 1860's*. London, 1927.

Briggs, Asa. *Victorian People: A Reassessment of Persons and Themes 1851-67*. London, 1954; Chicago, 1970.

Briggs, Asa. *Victorian Cities*. London, 1963.

Cunnington, C. Willett. *Feminine Attitudes in the Nineteenth Century*. London, 1955.

Cunnington, C. Willett. *English Women's Clothing in the 19th Century*. London, 1937.

Dodds, J. W. *The Age of Paradox: A Biography of England 1841-1851*. London, 1953.

Fischel and Boehn. *Modes and Manners of the XIX Century*. London, 1927.

Frazer, James George. *The Golden Bough, A Study in Magic and Religion*. London: Macmillian & Co. Ltd., 1951.

Gernsheim, Helmut. *Victoria R.: A Biography*. New York: Putnam, 1959.

Gloag, John. *Victorian Taste*. London, 1962.

Harrison, John F. C. *The Early Victorians 1832-51*. London: Panther Book Ltd., 1973.

Martin, Paul. *Victorian Snapshots*. With an introduction by Charles Harvard. London, 1939.

Pritchard, H. Baden. *The Studios of Europe*. New York: E. & H. T. Anthony & Co., 1882.

Strasser, Alex. *Victorian Photography—being an album of yesterday's camera-work by William Henry Fox Talbot, David Octavius Hill, Julia Margaret Cameron, Roger Fenton and others*. London, 1942.

Trevelyan, G. M. *English Social History*, Part 4. London, 1948.

Young, G. M. *Victorian England*. London, 1936.

Glossary

Albumen print: The most usual method of obtaining prints from wet collodion glass negatives. Paper which had been treated with white of egg (albumen) could be purchased. This paper was immersed in a solution of common salt for a few minutes and then dried. The paper was sensitized by floating the sized surface on a solution of silver nitrate. After drying in the dark the paper was ready to use. Albumen prints were dark brown or bronze but were often toned to a sepia color with chloride of gold solution. The process was introduced by L. D. Blanquart-Evrard in 1850.

Ambrotype: The American term for the glass collodion positive.

Calotype process: The only negative process in use before 1851, discovered by W. H. F. Talbot in September 1840. Writing paper was washed with silver nitrate solution on one side only and dried. It was then placed in a solution of potassium iodide for a few minutes. After washing again and drying, the iodized paper could be kept any length of time if it was not exposed to light. When the paper was required for use, it was treated with a solution of silver nitrate, gallic acid, and acetic acid (known as gallonitrate of silver). The sensitive paper was exposed in bright sunlight. The image was brought out on paper by washing it once more with water and fixed with solutions of potassium bromide or sodium thiosulphate. Positives were made from the negatives by the photogenic drawing process (without development).

Carte-de-visite: An albumen silver print (2¼″ x 3½″) popularized by Disderi of Paris in 1859, at first intended to supplement visiting cards.

150

Collodion: Made by dissolving gun-cotton in ether containing a small quantity of alcohol.

Daguerreotype process: The process disclosed by Daguerre in 1839 and consisting of five stages. (1) Thin sheets of silver, plated on copper, were polished or buffed; (2) the plate was sensitized by exposing it to the action of iodine vapor, and (3) then exposed to light in a camera; (4) the image was developed with mercury vapor and (5) fixed by washing the plate in a solution of common salt.

Dry plate: The first method of preparing plates which could be used dry, devised by the French chemist J. M. Taupenot in 1855. These plates, which were much slower than wet collodion plates, were not used for portraiture until much later.

Fixing: The process of making the image permanent. John Herschel suggested the use of "hypo" (sodium thiosulphate) instead of common salt for fixing the photographic image shortly after the daguerreotype process was disclosed, and this practice was soon generally adopted.

Glass collodion positive: Cheap imitation of the daguerreotype which it superseded. A glass collodion negative when mounted in front of a black surface appears to be a positive, particularly when the negative is underexposed or when the negative image is whitened by treatment with mecuric chloride. In England pictures made by this process were known as collodion positives; in America, ambrotypes.

Glass-house: Studio made of glazed blue glass, usually on the roof of a building, used during the first thirty years in photography's history to provide adequate light for portrait photography. The first glass-house was erected by Richard Beard, in 1841, on the roof of the Royal Polytechnic Institution in London.

Photogenic drawing process: The first process to give fixed negatives, used by Fox Talbot from his first experiments in 1834, until he discovered the possibility of developing the latent image in September 1840. Good quality writing paper was dipped into a weak solution of common salt and wiped dry. A solution of silver nitrate in then applied to one surface only and the paper is dried. The paper can then be exposed in a camera and a negative image will be obtained after 30 to 90 minutes. The image was fixed with a saturated solution of common salt. Photogenic drawings may have lilac, pink, or yellow images, depending on the fixative used.

Printing frame: The apparatus used after 1855 for making positive prints from negatives. It was usually constructed of mahogany and fitted with a glass plate front.

The back is divided centrally lengthwise and closed by two battens, fitted on the underside with steel springs.

Printing-out: Making a positive print from a negative, with no development stage, as with wet collodion process. Paper, usually albumen paper, was exposed beneath the negative in a printing-frame until an image appeared.

Salted paper positives: Paper impregnated with common salt was sensitized before use by immersion in silver nitrate solution. Because of the ease of preparation, salted paper was the most usual method of producing paper positives up to about 1854, when it was replaced by the albumen process.

Stereoscopy: The impression of solidity obtained by viewing two pictures each presenting the same subject from a slightly different viewpoint, first used in photography in the early 1840s.

Talbotype process: The term often used to refer to the calotype process. Talbot named his invention the "calotype" after the Greek *kalos*, meaning beautiful.

Tinting: The technique for applying color, usually pastels, to photographs, suggested by Richard Beard in 1840.

Union case: Until the turn of the century used for protecting and presenting photographs. The case consisted of a mixture of shellac and papier-maché or sawdust, heated and pressed into a mold, which was usually based on the design of a popular painting. When the mixture was cooled, the fine detail of the dye was retained into the hardened compound. Union cases were of American origin, but were adopted in Britain in the 1840s.

Waxed paper negative: Gustave Le Gray introduced this modification of the calotype process in 1850. The thin paper was waxed by placing it on blotting paper on a heated metal box and rubbing wax into the surface. The process gave finer detail than the calotype process, but since the time of exposure was many minutes, it was not suitable for portraiture.

Index∗

∗Page numbers in italics refer to illustrations.